HOW TO BREAK FREE OF THE DRAMA TRIANGLE AND VICTIM CONSCIOUSNESS

Barry K. Weinhold, PhD

Janae B. Weinhold, PhD

PUBLISHED BY:
CICRCL Press
Colorado Springs CO

CICRCL Press: A Division of the Colorado Institute for Conflict Resolution & Creative Leadership, a Colorado nonprofit, tax-exempt Corporation.

Copyright 2017
Barry K. Weinhold, PhD & Janae B. Weinhold, PhD
ISBN 10: 1499100299
ISBN-13: 978-1499100297

Email: cicrcl@bellsouth.net
We'd love to hear how this book has helped you.
For more information about the Weinholds' work and other books, go to: www.weinholds.org

ACKNOWLEDGEMENTS

This book grew out of our many personal experiences with the Drama Triangle, and our professional experiences of teaching students and counseling clients struggling with victim consciousness. From these life experiences, we identified the developmental sources that create the Drama Triangle and the life-limiting nature of victim consciousness.

We also acknowledge our children and family members who helped us hone our awareness of Drama Triangle dynamics and victim consciousness, and taught us the "fine points" about exiting the Triangle.

Thank you to our families, students, and clients for teaching us, and to the numerous individuals who have contributed their editorial comments and proofing of this manuscript.

CONTENTS

PART TWO
HOW TO BREAK FREE OF THE DRAMA TRIANGLE

INTRODUCTION

We wrote this book because we believe that the Drama Triangle and Victim Consciousness are at the core of a social and cultural matrix that blocks both our personal growth as individuals and our collective evolution as a species. We also believe that breaking free of the Drama Triangle and Victim Consciousness is the fastest way to shift your consciousness and claim your personal power. We say this because it has been our personal experience and that of many of our clients.

What is Victim Consciousness? Here's the short 'n' sweet definition: It's when life happens *to* you rather than <u>you</u> actively participating in making life happen. It is more than just an attitude; it is how you live your life.

Victim Consciousness involves a set of beliefs and feelings learned in your family of origin. Developmentally, it is the result of trauma during the separation stage between two and three years of age. We could say, "It's wired into you." However, once you become aware about the cause of this distorted thinking, you can change the thoughts, feelings and beliefs that trap you in Victim Consciousness.

The inventory below will help you identify the beliefs and feelings that contribute to your Drama Triangle dynamics and Victim Consciousness.

DRAMA TRIANGLE SELF-INVENTORY:

On a scale of 1 to 4, indicate how frequently these beliefs influence how you think about yourself and others.

Key: 1 = Hardly Ever; 2 = Sometimes; 3 = Frequently; 4 = Almost Always.

_____ 1.   It is my fault when someone gets angry with me.
_____ 2.   Other people's feelings/needs are more important than mine.
_____ 3.   People will think I am too aggressive if I express my feelings/needs directly.
_____ 4.   I worry about how others may respond when I state my feelings or needs.

_____ 5. I have to walk on eggshells so I don't do something that causes people to get angry with me or abandon me.

_____ 6. I have to give up my needs in my relationships so people will want to be with me.

_____ 7. I must be perfect so that others will love me and not abandon me.

_____ 8. I rely on others to make important decisions.

_____ 9. I hold back when reacting to what others say and do, rather than saying what I believe.

_____ 10. How I feel about myself depends on other people's opinions of me.

_____ 11. It's dangerous for me to ask directly for what I want or need from others.

_____ 12. I avoid assuming a position of responsibility.

_____ 13. When faced with a problem, I can only think of two conflicting solutions to the problem.

_____ 14. I need to make sure I meet other people's needs so they will like me and want to be with me.

_____ 15. It's best to seek out relationships where I can meet the needs of others and make them happy.

_____ 16. If I have to ask for what I want or need from loved ones, they don't love me enough to know what I need.

_____ 17. I have a difficult time knowing what I want or need.

_____ 18. I can't let others get too close to me or my life will be consumed by their needs.

_____ 19. I have difficulty in knowing how I really feel.

_____ 20. I exaggerate my accomplishments when I meet someone new so they will like me.

_____ 21. If people knew who I really was, they would not want to be with me.

_____ 22. I'm afraid people will find out that I'm not who they think I am.

_____ 23. I can't ask other people for help even when I need it because they will think I am too needy.

_____ 24. I feel controlled by what others expect of me.

_____ 25. I feel it is really important for me to have the "right answers" or others will think I am stupid.

_____ 26. I can't admit to a mistake because I am afraid people might reject me if I did.

_____ 27. I reject offers of help from others, even when I need them.

_____ 28. I compare myself to others because I feel either one-up or one-down in relation to them.

_____ 29.   I feel hurt when others don't recognize my accomplishments.

_____ 30.   I don't deserve to be loved by others.

_____   **TOTAL SCORE**

Interpretation of scores:

30 – 50 = Few beliefs that contribute to the Drama Triangle in your life.

51 – 80 = Some beliefs that contribute to the Drama Triangle in your life.

81+ =   Many beliefs that contribute to the Drama Triangle in your life.

Note: The items you answered as "3 or 4" have the most control over you.

You can see why these beliefs keep you trapped in Victim Consciousness! We view this dynamic as a delayed developmental stage in which people don't take responsibility for what happens to them, whether it's <u>good or bad</u>.

If something *good* happens, then people believe they were just lucky. If it is something *bad*, they believe it's someone else's fault. In this belief structure, there's no personal accountability requiring people either to self-reflect or self-correct.

People with Victim Consciousness think in black-and-white terms and see only two choices when they have problems. Victim Consciousness also contains attitudes of helplessness, powerlessness and hopelessness.

What is the Drama Triangle? It's a dysfunctional social game involving three interchangeable roles: Victim, Rescuer and Persecutor. It's often an underlying plot in soap operas, sit-coms, television dramas and movies. There is always the villain, the victim and the hero. In this book we describe how this social game works, its social consequences, and how to break free of the Drama Triangle.

STAGES OF CONSCIOUSNESS

The research of Robert Kegan helped us better understand *Victim Consciousness*. His books, *The Emerging Self* (1982) and *In Over Our Heads* (1997), discuss adult trials and tribulations, and identify five stages of consciousness.

In his research, Kegan interviewed thousands of adult subjects —mostly college sophomores. He found more than 70 percent of them either felt like victims or were actively trying to victimize others. Then he reviewed other research studies and found similar results.

In Over Our Heads identifies five distinct stages of development and the approximate percentage of the population that is in each stage. Here are the stages Kegan identified and some of the characteristics of each.

STAGE ONE: MAGICAL THINKING. People in this stage lack good cause-and-effect thinking and often attribute the things that happen to them as "magical." They often act on their impulses and engage in fantasy projections. They typically blame conflicts on coincidence, someone or something else, or on a situation that actually has little to do with the source of the problem.

STAGE TWO: CONCRETE THINKING. In this stage, people base their reality on what is tangible, visible and concrete. They are not able to understand abstract concepts such as justice or freedom. Things must be presented to them in concrete and quantifiable ways. They want to address only the most visible and obvious aspects of conflicts, as the rest seem unimportant to them.

STAGE THREE: CROSS-RELATIONAL THINKING. People in this stage are able to think abstractly. They can see relationships between categories of information, but still tend to see the world as acting *upon* them. For this reason they often think, act, sound and feel like victims. Because they use either-or thinking, they typically find themselves in victim – victimizer dynamics during conflict situations.

STAGE FOUR: SYSTEMIC THINKING. These people are able to think holistically and recognize the underlying patterns of thoughts, feelings and behaviors that repeat in their lives and control them in some way. They are able to relate current conflicts to similar unresolved conflicts from their past. They can understand why a conflict might recur because something from their past contributes to it.

STAGE FIVE: TRANS-SYSTEMIC THINKING. People in this stage recognize the correlations between their current conflicts and unresolved conflicts and issues from their past. They also have the ability to recognize windows of opportunity that allow them to make different choices —choices that will change patterns that might be restricting them. People in this stage are able to make cause-and-effect correlations, which allow them to resolve intractable conflicts at their source.

Based on his research, and review of other research about these stages, Kegan estimated about 70% of adults were operating at Stage Three or below.

Approximately 30% were entering or at Stage Four, and less than 1% were entering or at Stage Five.

Kegan also found in his research that 30% of adults were moving out of Stage Three's victim/victimizer consciousness. They were learning how to connect the dots between their behavior and the events that they experienced in their past. Gradually, this group was able to recognize the cause-and-effect principle at work in their lives — how certain choices and behaviors yielded predictable and consistent outcomes and results.

The bottom line, according to Kegan, was that people could learn to recognize how their behavior choices caused them to get trapped in Victim Consciousness. They were also able to recognize how unresolved childhood conflicts and dynamics contributed to their Victim Consciousness.

Kegan also found that those who were above Stage Three were more likely both to understand the impact of unresolved childhood conflicts on their lives and to free themselves from these dynamics. Here's an inventory to help you identify where you are in Kegan's stages of consciousness.

STAGES OF CONSCIOUSNESS INVENTORY

On a scale of 1 to 4, indicate how frequently these beliefs influence how you think about yourself and others.

Key: 1 = Hardly Ever; 2 = Sometimes; 3 = Frequently; 4 = Almost Always.

_____ 1.   Conflicts just seem to happen to me, and I have no idea why.

_____ 2.   In a conflict situation, someone has to win and someone has to lose.

_____ 3.   In a conflict situation, I feel victimized by the actions of others.

_____ 4.   I can see the underlying patterns in my recurring conflicts.

_____ 5.   I have the skills to help others successfully resolve their conflicts

_____ 6.   If I have a conflict, I turn it over to God or my higher power.

_____ 7.   In a conflict situation, I tend to see myself as right and the other person as wrong.

_____ 8.   In a conflict situation, I try to "shoot down" the arguments of the other person.

_____ 9.   As the result of resolving my conflicts, I am able to better understand myself and why I get into certain kinds of conflict.

_____ 10. I have altered some of my values and beliefs as the result of my conflicts.

_____ 11. I wish the people who bug me would just go away.

_____ 12. In a conflict situation, I end up not getting what I want, and the other person does.

_____ 13. I lack confidence in my ability to resolve my conflicts successfully.

_____ 14. My current conflicts remind me of similar conflicts I had as a child growing up in my family.

_____ 15. I have the ability to locate and resolve any unresolved conflicts from my past.

_____ 16. In a conflict situation, I am afraid that I'll lose myself if I consider the other person's position or needs.

_____ 17. I believe that the past is the past; you have to put it behind you and go on.

_____ 18. I depend on the instruction of my teachers because they have more knowledge and experience than I do.

_____ 19. I am able to see how the patterns of unresolved conflicts from my past are controlling my life.

_____ 20. I am able to change the underlying dysfunctional patterns of behavior that have controlled my life.

Interpretation of Scores

Add the numbers for the four items in each stage.

Stage One: Add items 1, 6, 11, and 16   = _____

Stage Two: Add items 2, 7, 12, and 17   = _____

Stage Three: Add items 3, 8, 13, and 18   = _____

Stage Four: Add items 4, 9, 14, and 19   = _____

Stage Five: Add items 5, 10, 15, and 20   = _____

Rankings

10 – 16 = High SOC score for that stage.

5 – 9 =   Medium SOC score for that stage.

1 – 4 =   Low SOC score for that stage.

SPEAKING FROM OUR OWN EXPERIENCES

Our combined 60+ years of personal and professional experience working in our relationship, with our families, students and clients have helped us learn how to break free of the Drama Triangle and Victim Consciousness. Working on ourselves individually and within our relationships provided us with a "laboratory" to develop effective tools for identifying the sources of the Drama Triangle and for breaking free of Victim Consciousness.

Barry also conducted research in his graduate classes at the University of Colorado at Colorado Springs to test Kegan's findings on Stages of Consciousness. He wanted to determine if Kegan's research findings were characteristic of the graduate students he was teaching.

Barry designed and validated a paper/pencil test that he administered at the beginning of his graduate class in conflict resolution and then re-administered at the end. He also gave this test to a control group of graduate students at the same level who had not yet taken this course. This is the same SOC Inventory shown above.

Barry's pre-test results from students enrolled in his class paralleled Kegan's percentages, showing about 70% of them operating at or below Stage Three. The responses of the students on the post-test showed that many of them had moved out of the victim – victimizer stage into Stage Four. The change, when compared with the results of the Control group's scores, was highly significant. When polled about what contributed to this change, the students said it was the modeling he did as the instructor in the class, and that the content of the course allowed them to reflect upon their life experiences.

We encourage you to "take a journey" while reading this book. Take time to reflect upon your own life experiences, to identify places where you still feel life happens *to* you and traps you in Victim Consciousness. We encourage you to complete the inventories, look for opportunities to become more self-aware, and seek places where you can express more personal power in your life.

PART ONE

WHAT ARE THE DRAMA TRIANGLE AND VICTIM CONSCIOUSNESS?

CHAPTER ONE

OUR PERSONAL EXPERIENCES WITH THE DRAMA TRIANGLE & VICTIM CONSCIOUSNESS

"Sympathy for victims is always counter-balanced by an equal and opposite feeling of resentment towards them."

—*Ben Elton*

The Drama Triangle is an interpersonal communication dynamic so embedded in human consciousness and social interactions that we call it "the only game in town." We grappled with it unconsciously in our personal relationship when we first met. Eventually we recognized it as a dysfunctional social game that we learned growing up. We came to understand that hidden and unhealed childhood trauma drove this dynamic and recognized how it interfered with our efforts as adults to take responsibility for meeting our own needs.

We both grew up in families where no one asked directly for what they wanted or needed. We learned to use manipulation and indirectness to get others to give us what we wanted.

If it was comforting we needed, we got sick. We also figured out that we could get our needs met if we did things for others and obligated them to give us something back. While this kind of caretaking worked sometimes, it also created a crippling kind of codependency.

I (Barry) remember when I was about four years old I asked my mother for something I needed. She said, *"Don't be so selfish."* And when I was five years old, I remember my maternal grandmother saying to me, *"Be a good boy, and don't cause your parents any problems. They have enough troubles of their own.*" I didn't know what their problems were, but the message was, "*Don't ask for anything that might cause a problem for them.*"

I (Janae) learned that being direct about asking for what I wanted brought on the "pointy finger" and shaming statements. People said things like, "*Who do you think you are, the Queen of Sheba?*" Well, I had no idea who the Queen of Sheba was, but I knew acting like her and being direct wouldn't get me what I wanted. I was sufficiently oppositional as a child to risk such insults and push for attention to my needs. This, however, just turned into a power struggle with my parents.

Churches and religious organizations also trained us to get our needs met indirectly. Our Sunday school teachings contained admonitions such as, "*Think first about what God wants, then what others want, and lastly what you want.*" Our church experiences also implied that asking for what we wanted was being *selfish* and *ungodly*.

We also grew up with cultural and gender rules and roles that dictated how we should get our needs met. Boys could be more assertive than girls. Girls were not supposed to be direct about their needs. Barry never saw his father even cook oatmeal, so he expected to be cooked for when he got married. And Janae expected that she would have to do all the cooking.

At some point, the two of us realized that this social game-playing and dysfunctional communication created barriers in experiencing deeper intimacy. We each eventually recognized the unspoken expectations that we had for each other without having to ask. It was awful! We realized that our past Victim Consciousness experiences were pushing us to find ways to break free of these dysfunctional communication patterns.

We first noticed them when driving somewhere together as Barry automatically went to the driver's side and Janae to the passenger's side without any negotiations. We wondered, "How did it get decided who drives?" We started to see how many unconscious expectations we had because we hadn't learned how to negotiate and to ask directly for what we wanted.

As we began to understand the Drama Triangle game, we saw it everywhere — on television, in the movies, in politics. We saw how it caused recurring cycles of gridlock in Washington. There was always the Villain, the Victim, and the Rescuer.

As we observed what happened at the University of Colorado, where we both taught, we recognized the same dynamics. We also saw it in our national economy — capitalism itself seems to be based on the Drama Triangle.

4

And the political dramas in our government showed us how much this dynamic had permeated social structures.

I (Barry) saw the Drama Triangle play out over and over at the University during my 30 years there. Those who refused to play the Drama Triangle game got fewer rewards than those who learned to play the game well. Sometimes they were even punished!

Everyone in the University's hierarchical structure was expected to take care of the needs of those in the tier above them before meeting their own needs. The students were expected to take care of the needs of their professors; the professors made sure they met the needs of their department chairs or deans, and so on.

People were expected to take care of those above them on the chain of command. Notice that the students sat at the bottom of the hierarchy. They had no one below them to meet their needs. They were left to fend for themselves in this upside down hierarchy, which is why so many students struggle in school and eventually drop out.

We labeled this dynamic a *reversal process*. Rather than the older, larger, more capable and responsible tier caring for those in the younger, smaller, less capable and responsible tiers, it was reversed. It puzzled me why people — including myself — would accept this reversal process so readily and without any complaints.

When we thought about the early development of our clients, we realized that the reversal process was *familiar* — it begins in families. Parents often look into the eyes of their newborn child and fantasize how this child will eventually serve their needs. Perhaps they see the child becoming a doctor, lawyer, or scientist and doing something to make the parents look good.

These kinds of parents fail to see children as they actually are. Throughout early childhood, children are subtly programmed to meet their parents' unspoken physical, mental, emotional and spiritual needs rather than following their own inner rhythms, dreams and desires.

There are also the *good old boy/good old girl* games woven into businesses where organizations keep people stuck in game-playing systems. These systems use the Drama Triangle dynamics to create chaos, drama and help some people maintain control. We call this part of the Drama Triangle game the Need/Obligate System, and we discuss it and the reversal process in more detail in Chapter 8.

THE DRAMA TRIANGLE AND THE COLD WAR

Our final realization about the pervasiveness of the Drama Triangle came in 1990 when we first met with people from the former USSR. We were delegates at the first Soviet-American Citizen's Summit Conference in Washington, D.C.

There were about 400 Americans from all walks of life at the conference, and about 100 Soviet participants. We had lots of time to meet informally and talk with each other. At one point, we began sharing what it had been like living through the Cold War in each of our countries. What we learned was very interesting.

During the Cold War era, the USSR and the USA were both playing out Drama Triangle dynamics on international and political stages. The Soviets saw the USA as Persecutors with a global imperialistic goal to make the whole world capitalist. They saw the developing countries such as Vietnam and Nicaragua as Victims of our imperialism who needed Rescuing. They saw themselves as the Rescuers. We were shocked when we heard them say this!

Then we shared our very different perceptions about this international Cold War Drama Triangle. We talked about how the US government portrayed the USSR as Persecutors whose goal was to make the whole world communist. We believed Vietnam and Nicaragua, and other developing countries, were helpless victims who needed the US to rescue them from the USSR's aggression.

We still remember the deep silence that settled in after this exchange with our Soviet colleagues. It was so clear to all of us that the governments of both our countries had misled us and promoted seeing each other as "the enemy." It was a very sobering moment.

We were also a bit stunned by another aspect of this exchange. Initially we thought the Drama Triangle was a game that played out primarily in dysfunctional families. What flashed in front of us was a realization that *Uncle Sam* and *Mother Russia* were playing out a global dysfunctional family game. In this aha moment, we realized the Drama Triangle is the only game … on planet Earth!

The Drama Triangle is so common that people accept it as *just the way things are.* We know that unless people recognize Drama Triangle dynamics and understand its negative effects on their lives, they are likely to remain as Victims stuck in Victim Consciousness. We want everyone to understand how and why the Drama Triangle is so pervasive and the negative effects it has on our lives. In this book, we show you how you can break free of its grip on you, your loved ones, and your destiny.

CHAPTER TWO

THE HISTORY OF THE DRAMA TRIANGLE

"If I don't see myself as a victim, then I'm not a victim"

—*Noomi Rapace*

The term Drama Triangle was first identified as a social game in 1968 by Stephen Karpman, a psychiatrist who practiced Transactional Analysis (TA). In TA, a game is a social interaction containing a series of transactions that involve rotating roles and which moves toward an expected outcome.

Karpman recognized the game aspect of social interactions because of his interest in sports. He understood how coaches use diagrams to help players learn different offensive and defensive strategies.

So Karpman combined his interest in sports with TA founder Eric Berne's social game theory, and he came up with the Drama Triangle. Let's begin by identifying the criteria that define a social interaction as a TA game:

1. They involve a continuing series of complementary and reciprocal transactions that look like honest social interactions between people but are not.
2. They always have an ulterior or hidden transaction that contains the basic message of the game. There is a concealed message without an honest, straightforward social transaction.
3. There is a predictable payoff that ends the game. Usually this provides the game player with a justifiable reason to discharge feelings, to be irresponsible or to get ego needs met. Getting to the payoff is the purpose of playing the game.

GAMES PEOPLE PLAY

The founder of TA, Eric Berne, wrote *Games People Play* (1961), a best selling book in which he describes a number of mind games that people act out through a series of patterned and predictable social transactions. These transactions appear normal to bystanders or even to the people involved, but they are emotionally dishonest.

Ultimately, these games help people conceal their real motivations. Game transactions are also used as a form of manipulation, particularly against those who are naive. Berne's book uses casual, often humorous phrases to describe the themes in these dysfunctional games, such as:

See What You Made Me Do?
Why Don't You — Yes But.
Ain't It Awful?
Why Does Everything Always Happen to Me?
You Got Me Into This.
Look How Hard I've Tried.
I'm Only Trying to Help You.
Let's You and Him Fight.

The most interesting aspect of these adult games is that they are so child-like and can be found on any pre-school or elementary school playground.

Dr. Berne believed that adults play these games as a result of their warped childhood, society and culture. He recognized that most people are psychologically incapable of authentic intimacy. Because they don't know how to create and sustain intimacy in their closest relationships, they play these games instead.

They also enable players to feel and look good without actually excelling at anything. Berne believed that most of contemporary social life consists of game-playing rather than authentic emotional transactions. He and others say that about three out of every five social transactions involve some kind of game.

TRANSACTIONAL ANALYSIS AND GAMES

In the TA framework, players use games that give them permission to express difficult or forbidden emotions such as anger, resentment and superiority. Games also allow players to feel justified in doing or not doing certain behaviors that are normally seen as socially unacceptable.

TA mind-game players are not conscious of their actions, and therefore see themselves as innocent. They usually are unaware of their indirect interpersonal communication and how they project unwanted parts of themselves and their childhood wounds onto others. For example, a person who grew up being dominated will often dominate others. The abused become the abusers.

Mind games also create artificial social environments that prevent people from expressing genuine adult emotions and appropriate, authentic, social responses. These psychological games, which are not actually played for fun, are similar to real strategic games, such as chess or monopoly.

Social game players learn the rules by watching others and by participating; no one actually sits children down and teaches them how to play these games. Whenever people interact with each other, you will find them playing these mind games. All around the world, social mind games form the most important aspect of human social life. Some are quite functional and some are very dysfunctional.

Many fairy tales are actually cultural stories based on mind games that people have played since time immemorial. Some examples of fairy tales based on mind games are *Cinderella, Beauty and the Beast, The Emperor's New Clothes, Snow White and the Seven Dwarfs, Peter Pan, Rapunzel,* and *The Spider and the Fly.* It's interesting that the Cinderella fairy tale is found in some form or another in virtually every culture in the world.

Mythology also contains these game dynamics. The Greeks acted out their myths in the form of tragedies and comedies. The main difference between a fairy tale and a myth is that in myths, gods and goddesses are also players.

Mind games have existed for most of recorded history, which is why they are so deeply rooted in our psyches, and why it is so difficult to break free from them and the Victim Consciousness they create.

EXAMPLES OF TA GAMES THAT USE THE DRAMA TRIANGLE

NIGYSOB (nigy-sob) is a great example of a Persecutor game. The acronym stands for "Now I've got you, you son of a bitch." In this Persecutor game the objective or payoff is revenge and domination. For example, A hired B to do a plumbing job. B underestimated the price of a $3 part as $1 on

A's $300 job. A objects to B's $302 bill and refuses to pay any of it because of the additional $2 charge for the part. A has an excuse to get angry and hold B hostage. A demands that B absorb the $2 error, instead of just paying A what he owes him — $302.

I Am Only Trying to Help is a Rescuer game in which one person tries to help another either unnecessarily or without being asked. This one-up game is designed to make a Rescuer person look kind and helpful.

In reality, the Rescuer is satisfying some personal ego need to look and feel superior to others. The Rescuer wants to believe others are weak and unable to take care of themselves, and they need the help of someone who is stronger or smarter.

Ain't it Awful? ? is a Victim game that supports suffering. Some Victims unconsciously seek out suffering like a kind of precious gift. These Victims unconsciously feel grateful for people or situations that cause them misfortune. A common scenario in this game involves a failed Rescue. Then these Victims can feel bad and get the payoff — suffering — because they believe no one really understands or cares about them.

A nation that is steeped in Victim Consciousness, for example, will continue to support incompetent leaders and a corrupt government. When citizens vote in crooks, liars and con artists, and things go wrong, they can gather in public and private places to complain and whine, playing the *Ain't it Awful* game.

These people make no conscious effort to take responsible action, seek alternatives, or support leaders who don't cheat and lie, and thus eliminate their suffering. Their payoff is suffering and getting attention by complaining about how bad things are. They want things to stay bad so they have something to complain about.

THE DRAMA TRIANGLE ROLES

The Drama Triangle game has three rotating roles: Victim, Persecutor and Rescuer. Each role has specific behaviors, beliefs, perceptions and payoffs.

THE PERSECUTOR ROLE

Games: *NIGYSOB*, *It's All Your Fault*, and *See What You Made Me Do*.

The Persecutor is the bad-guy role in the Drama Triangle. Most people avoid it unless they have a need to vent "justified" negative feelings such as anger or rage. In these instances, they must identify some excuse to feel justified or right so they can express their negative feelings. Once they have a good reason for making someone bad, they can dump their repressed feelings. This is one of the Persecutor payoffs. Righteous indignation, the most common form of Persecutor behavior, puts others down by using guilt and shame. Here's a summary of the Persecutor role.

- Sets unnecessarily restrictive rules and limits.
- Blames others for whatever happens.
- Criticizes all actions of others.
- Keeps the Victim oppressed.
- Expresses justified and righteous anger.
- Uses guilt and shame to put another person down.
- Provokes conflict and drama.
- Takes a rigid, authoritative stance.
- Acts and sounds like a Critical Parent.
- Comes from an *I'm okay/good, you're not okay/bad position.*

The Payoff: They get to be right and therefore justified in releasing pent-up emotions. The Persecutor role allows a player to remain in control and dominate others. When someone rejects the heavy-handed behavior and expresses justified anger in return, this catapults them into the Victim and Victim Consciousness.

THE RESCUER ROLE

Games: *I Am Only Trying to Help You* , and *Look How Hard I've Tried.*

The Rescuer is the good-guy role in the Drama Triangle. It provides rescuers with a look-good opportunity to get their ego needs met. Rescuing allows people to look important, and competent, and to feel superior. Rescuer's acts are often accompanied with woeful messages of self-sacrifice and martyrdom, which also obligate the Victim in some way.

The Rescuer's attempts to help someone usually fail in some critical way, which then gives the Victim permission to get angry. This is how people can quickly switch roles — the Victim moves into the Persecutor role and attacks the Rescuer. The Rescuer then switches into the Victim role, saying indignantly, *"But I was only trying to help you!"*

13

We discovered that most Rescuers are often acting out their own unmet need in the past to be rescued. They unconsciously project this need from hidden and unhealed childhood trauma and then use it to justify rescuing others. Here's a summary of the Rescuer role.

- Feels obligated to rescue, often really not wanting to.
- Does things for others that they don't ask for and are able to do for themselves.
- Feels guilty if they don't help others.
- Acts and sounds like an Authoritative Parent, keeping the Victim dependent and helpless with their Rescuing.
- Supports the Victim's perception of being weak and a failure.
- Expects to fail in his or her own attempt to Rescue the Victim.
- Avoids conflict and drama, often behaving like a pleasing, marshmallow person.
- Comes from an *I'm okay/good, you're bad/not okay position.*

Payoff: Get to look okay, strong and capable, and be one-up. Ultimate Payoff: Become a Victim when their attempts to help others don't work.

VICTIM ROLE

Games: *Poor Me*, and *Ain't It Awful.*

The Victim role is key in the Drama Triangle because the whole game revolves around competing to be the Victim. It is the one role whose needs can be met without having to ask others directly. Victims don't have to take responsibility for their behavior or feelings. They blame whatever isn't working in their lives on someone or something else.

There are two types of Victims: the Pathetic Victim and the Angry Victim. The Pathetic Victim plays one-down games, holds pity-parties, displays woeful, poor-me facial expressions and body language, and shows one-down verbal language.

The Angry Victim pretends to be powerful, using guilt and shame to get others to feel sorry for them. The underlying motive of the Angry Victim is revenge. Both types want someone to blame for their feelings and troubles. Always operating in the background, of course, is the desire to attract a Rescuer who will take care of them. Here's a summary of the Victim role.

- Feels victimized, oppressed, helpless, hopeless, powerless and ashamed.
- Looks for a Rescuer to help perpetuate negative self-beliefs.
- Uses the Victim role to avoid making decisions, solving problems and taking responsibility.
- Uses conflict situations to play Victim.
- Embraces or creates conflict situations.
- Has a slouched, dejected body posture.
- Operates from an *I'm not okay/bad, you're okay/good position.*

Payoff: They get their wants and needs met without asking.

Martyrs are a special class of Victims. Sometimes described as emotional vampires, they act out toxic, theatrical vignettes that escalate into hysteria and high drama in order to get what they want.

Martyrs use their Victim status to invoke extreme pity and to prove that nothing can improve their situation. Rather than blame other people for their troubles, they blame them on God or some other omnipotent force. Martyrs are the most eloquent and committed kind of Victim.

The *drama* part of the Triangle comes from the fact that game-players rotate roles. They typically start out in the Rescuer role but end up as the Victim. This rapid role switching confuses people. It disrupts their attempts to think logically and to express their authentic emotions. In dysfunctional families, this plays out as the *talk fast, don't listen* game.

Effective Drama Triangle players must become adept at rapidly switching roles if they are to create confusion in their social interactions. They switch roles quickly, defend and protect themselves, and deny responsibility by using the Three Rules of Chaos:

- Make a game out of everything,
- Deny everything, and
- Blame others for everything to put them on the defensive.

The faster the roles change on the Triangle, the more the drama increases. As people's brains short out, they become increasingly frustrated and angry. At some point the emotional intensity peaks. Then players can express rage, scream, lose control of their emotions, and maybe even get violent.

According to Berne, there are first-degree games that just involve making someone uncomfortable. Second-degree games involve threatening someone's safety. Third-degree games can be life-threatening. While the Drama Triangle can be played at any of these three degrees, they often begin at the first degree but can escalate to second or third degree.

WHAT KEEPS THE GAME GOING?

Competition for the Victim role keeps the game going. Let us repeat this. *It is competition for the Victim role that keeps the Drama Triangle game going.*

Each player secretly strategizes ways to claim the Victim role. It is the prize! Only here can you get others to meet your needs without having to ask directly, and blame others when things don't work out.

The Persecutor initially feels righteous in expressing anger at the Victim, but then may feel guilty after attacking someone who is weak and helpless. The Victim can then push the Persecutor's "guilty" button, blaming them for a lack of compassion or appreciation for the Victim's challenging problems. Then the Angry Victim is justified in turning the Persecutor's anger back on them. This act of revenge flips the Persecutor into the Victim role. What a merry-go-round!

The Rescuer may also secretly envy all the attention the Victim gets without having to be accountable. The Rescuer's unconscious envy and associated ego wounds are often related to their own need to be taken care of and to get attention.

This unconscious yearning to be cared for often provokes the Rescuer into doing or saying something that causes the Victim to collapse. This may motivate the Angry Victim to switch to the Persecutor role, where they express their anger at the Rescuer for failing to do they said they would. The Rescuer then collapses and gets to be the new Victim, which is where the Rescuer secretly wanted to be. Then the Rescuer exclaims, "Don't blame me, I was only trying to help you!"

If you are feeling confused after reading about players' rapid role-switching, their unconscious agendas and the associated chaos ... welcome home! This is exactly how it feels when you are playing on the Triangle and being flipped out of one role and into another.

CHAPTER THREE

HOW THE DRAMA TRIANGLE
MIND GAME WORKS

*"Persecutors fear loss of control. Rescuers fear loss
of purpose. Rescuers need Victims—someone to
protect or fix— to bolster their self-esteem."*

—David Emerson

The Drama Triangle mind game is described in Transactional Analysis as a series of rotating behavioral roles that people learn in their family of origin. Drama Triangle mind games play out in groups of people who operate in Victim Consciousness as Victims, Persecutors or Rescuers. People who play on the Drama Triangle go either one-up or one-down in their relationships. The Drama Triangle allows them to switch between one-up and one-down positions. The Rescuer and Persecutor roles are one-up positions, and the Victim role is a one-down position.

The game involves a series of convoluted power and control games that help players get different needs met without having to transact them directly. For this reason, the coveted role in the Victim!

Once you understand the Drama Triangle, you will immediately recognize many different places where its dynamic operates. You'll see it at work, while you are watching TV, reading a novel, shopping in the grocery store, driving in traffic, or just having a meal with your family. It's everywhere!

In dysfunctional families, asking directly for what you want or need often provokes shaming and name-calling by parents or other family members. This is because the Drama Triangle game contains an underlying, twisted belief in deprivation: there is not enough _____ to go around. It may be Mother's love, Father's attention, money or loving kindness.

If you ASK for this "something," you'll likely be accused of breaking the unspoken rule about never asking. As soon as you break this rule, parents or other family members will accuse you of being selfish and/or self-centered.

Asking directly for someone to help you meet your needs, for example, is taboo in the game. Either you learn to do without the something, or you have to figure out an indirect way to get it. This is the core of the Drama Triangle: an indirect relational dynamic for getting something that is perceived to be scarce.

Karpman created the diagram below to show how the Drama Triangle works:

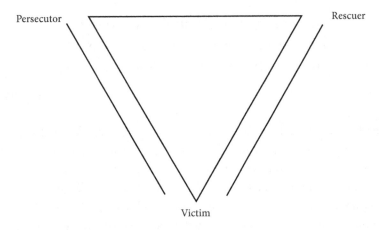

- The persecutor and Victim interact.
- The Rescuer and the Victim interact.
- The Persecutor and the Rescuer do not interact.

You can see in this diagram that there is no direct communication link between the Persecutor and the Rescuer. Since the Rescuer and Persecutor are competing for the Victim role on the Triangle, they don't interact with each other.

Any time there is a two-way interaction or transaction and one of the three people is out of the loop, the two-against-one thing occurs and it's known as triangulating.

AN EXAMPLE OF A FAMILY DRAMA TRIANGLE

Here's an example of Drama Triangle dynamics that involves two parents and three children. You can think about this tale as family theater, with regular and predictable changes in the roles and characters.

Act One. Dad comes home from work to find his children in the family room watching television and eating snacks. Mom is in the kitchen drinking a cup of coffee and reading the newspaper.

This domestic scene does not match the expectations that Dad had on his drive home. He fantasized that the house would be quiet, the children would be in their rooms doing homework, and Mom would have dinner prepared and maybe a cold drink waiting for him.

When Dad opens the front door, he finds things are not as he imagined. He assumes the Persecutor role when he vents his pent up frustrations from work at the children. *"You're supposed to be in your rooms doing your homework! You know the rules!"*

The children look up from the television, stunned by Dad's sharp tone. Feeling Persecuted by Father, they respond as Victims. "Well, Mom said it was okay for us to watch TV." Mother comes to the living room after hearing the raised voices, and the children they look to their Mother for help. She assumes to the Rescuer role when she says to Dad, *"The kids were just relaxing after being at school all day!"* This is the end of Act One.

Act Two. The second act opens at the point where Mother moves from the Rescuer to the Persecutor role and attacks Dad, *"Why do you have to come home every night and yell at the kids?"* Father then rotates into the Victim role, and the children quickly pick up the Rescuer role. They turn off the television and say, *"We're going to our rooms to do our homework."* End of Act Two.

Act Three. Dad shifts to the Persecutor role and attacks Mother, *"Why in the heck did you let the kids watch TV? And why don't you have dinner ready? What have you been doing since you got home from work? You knew I'd be hungry!"* Mother now rotates into the Victim role. Daughter hears her parents arguing in the kitchen, and she comes running in to Rescue. *"I'll help you get dinner ready, Mom."* End of Act Three.

Act Four. Dad, sensing that he looks like the bad guy, tries Rescue by saying, *"Why don't we just order a pizza or something and not worry about getting dinner ready?"*

Act Five. Mom, who hasn't yet been the Victim, overrides Dad's Victim effort by claiming the Super Victim or Martyr role. She says, *"I'm perfectly capable of getting dinner. Besides, it's too late for pizza. I already defrosted the meat for dinner and we can't afford to let it go to waste."* End of Act Five.

Act Six. Mother switches into the Persecutor role and Dad to the Victim when she says to him, *"All you can think of is something that is going to cost us more money. You don't ever pitch in and help get dinner ready. You just complain about its not being ready."* End of Act Six.

Act Seven. At this point Dad can shift to either Victim or Super Persecutor. He decides to rage and explodes into Persecutor so he can vent even more of his feelings from his frustrating day. *"I'm tired of always being the bad guy. I'm going to go and watch TV. I don't even want any dinner."* He then withdraws to the family room as the Angry Victim.

You can see in this domestic version of the Drama Triangle game how the three roles switched and players were able to get the payoffs associated with each. With the rotating roles and merry-go-round nature of the Drama Triangle, you see that the game could go on forever. In some families, it does.

CULTURAL SUPPORT FOR THE DRAMA TRIANGLE

We discovered a lot of cultural support for Drama Triangle dynamics in country music lyrics. Here are some actual Country and Western song titles that support the Angry Victim and the Sad/Pathetic Victim roles:

I Don't Know Whether to Kill Myself or Go Bowling
I Just Bought a Car from the Guy Who Stole My Girl, but the Car Don't Run So I Figure We Got An Even Deal
Here's a Quarter, Call Someone Who Cares
I Would Have Written You a Letter But I Couldn't Spell Yuck!
I'm Just a Bug on the Windshield of Life
I've Been Flushed from the Bathroom of Your Heart
I Don't Know Whether to Go Home or Go Crazy
I'm So Miserable Without You, It's Like Having You Here
If Drinkin' Don't Kill Me, Her Memory Will
If Love Were Oil, I'd Be a Quart Low
My Wife Ran Off with My Best Friend and I Sure Do Miss Him
She Got the Gold Mine and I Got the Shaft"
She Made Toothpicks Out of the Timber of My Heart

HOW TO BREAK FREE OF THE DRAMA TRIANGLE
AND VICTIM CONSCIOUSNESS

You're Out Doing What I'm Here Doing Without
Tennis Must Be Your Racket Cause Love Means Nothing to You
The Last Word in Lonesome Is Me
Learning to Live Again Without You Is Killing Me
You Done Tore Out My Heart and Stomped that Sucker Flat
You Hurt the Love Right Out of Me
You Are Ruining My Bad Reputation
You're The Reason the Kids Are So Ugly
You're a Cross I Can't Bear
You Can't Have Your Kate and Edith Too
Her Cheating Heart Made a Drunken Fool Out of Me

CHAPTER FOUR

DEVELOPMENTAL SOURCES OF THE DRAMA TRIANGLE & VICTIM CONSCIOUSNESS

"It is very difficult for people to believe the simple fact that every persecutor was once a victim. Yet it should be very obvious that someone who was allowed to feel free and strong from childhood does not have the need to humiliate another person."

—*Alice Miller*

Our research in developmental psychology and traumatology reveals that people who've experienced some form of physical or emotional abuse or neglect during the first three years of life are likely to have problems with intimacy in their adult relationships. Our books, *Breaking Free of the Codependency Trap* and *The Flight From Intimacy*, explain how a failure to complete essential developmental tasks during these first three years interferes with later development.

If the developmental tasks of bonding and separation were not completed on schedule, as they rarely are, they are waiting to be completed in your intimate adult relationships. This can cause many conflicts in your intimate adult relationships. We also know this personally, as we both had a lot of abuse and neglect during our early childhood development.

What we found is that relational or developmental trauma during the bonding and separation stages of development (birth – 36 months, the codependent and counter-dependent stages), has lifelong impact. This early trauma causes people to split the world into good and bad components. If they don't move through the splitting phase of the separation stage, they get stuck in black-and-white thinking and struggle with effective problem-solving as adults.

As adults they see only either/or solutions to their problems, which keeps them stuck in Victim Consciousness. They lack the ability to generate solutions that move them into both/and thinking, usually involving three or move possible solutions to the problem. This inability to move beyond either/or thinking is known as "splitting."

Developmentally, toddlers naturally split the world into good and bad — particularly in their interactions with their mothers. Splitting naturally occurs between 18 and 24 months of age. When their Mother is available to meet their needs, she is seen as the good mother. When she is not available to meet their needs in a timely and appropriate manner, she is the bad mother. The same is true of their perception of their Father.

With patience and the appropriate parental support, toddlers grow through the splitting stage and come to see their mother and father as having both good and bad qualities. This is how "both/and" thinking develops.

If children don't get the appropriate support for developing both/and thinking, they compensate for by playing social games where people are seen as either good or bad. The Drama Triangle is a good vs. bad game.

Thomas Harris, MD, another TA practitioner, recognized the role of splitting in social interactions. He wrote about it in his book, *I'm OK, You're OK,* (1967) one of the highest selling self-help books ever published. Harris described four "life positions" that people take on:

- I'm Not OK, You're OK
- I'm Not OK, You're Not OK
- I'm OK, You're Not OK
- I'm OK, You're OK

The most common position is *I'm Not OK, You're OK.* This occurs because children perceive adults as large, strong and competent, and themselves as little, weak and inept. They conclude, *I'm Not OK, and You're OK.* Parents, teachers and authority figures often reinforce this message.

Children who are physically or emotionally abused often conclude *I'm Not OK, You're Not OK* or *I'm OK, You're Not OK.* Harris' goal was to help people understand how their life position affects their communications and social transactions.

Compartmentalized either/or thinking is a major contributor to triangulation and Drama Triangle dynamics. Much of the splitting and drama revolves around the perpetual question of who is good and who is bad. Splitting also causes people to rotate between the Persecutor, Rescuer and Victim roles. It is like the *passing the hot potato game*. Splitting behaviors also form the foundation for lose-lose and win-lose styles of conflict resolution in adulthood.

Dysfunctional Drama Triangle experiences heavily imprint children's cognition. They create a twisted belief in children's minds that the only way they can get their needs met is by becoming Victims. As we said earlier, this makes the Victim role the most coveted.

Parents who use Drama Triangle dynamics to get their own needs met will find it very difficult to help their children move beyond the splitting phase of their development. This also prevents children from developing a sense of self between the ages of eight months and three years, and from becoming emotionally and psychologically separate from their parents.

Rather than developing a strong sense of internal power and self-directedness, these children learn to take their cues from others. They develop passive, other-directed, dependent relational behaviors that feed into the Victim role and prime them for playing social games such as the Drama Triangle. The best definition of a Victim is someone who is waiting for something bad to happen to them ... and it usually does.

TRAUMA AND THE DRAMA TRIANGLE

Drama Triangle dynamics in families are a primary cause of childhood trauma. Children who are repeatedly victimized during family conflicts, or who witness others being victimized, internalize these experiences. Their brains file situation-specific pictures, words, thoughts and feelings related to Drama Triangle experiences. This is the core definition of trauma.

These early, reality-shaping experiences create sensory memory modules that include images, smells, vocal tones, facial expressions, body memories, relational dynamics and situation-specific emotions. All are stored in children's brains and nervous systems to help them survive. Each memory module has specific triggers or cues stored in the central nervous system which are associated with these dramatic and traumatic experiences.

When a present-time event triggers these sensory memory modules from the past, it quickly catapults people into flashbacks where they re-experience memories. Their awareness is no longer in present time. Instead, they regress and are thrown back into the past to re-live the memory of an unresolved trauma.

What we describe is actually the criteria for diagnosing someone with post–traumatic stress disorder (PTSD). Later in this book, we will share some of our very effective methods for healing any developmental traumas you might still be carrying.

CHAPTER FIVE

POWER AND POWERLESSNESS ISSUES

"Revenge is not always sweet.
Once it is consummated, we feel inferior to our victim."

—Emile M. Cioran.

A differential in personal power is a major cause of Drama Triangle dynamics. There is always a perceived power difference between the Victim and the Persecutor, and between the Victim and the Rescuer.

Individuals or groups that have been dominated and see themselves as powerless and helpless have typically learned to operate from a Victim stance. If they feel powerless and want to feel more powerful, they Rescue others in order to be one-up on them. This strategy usually backfires, and they get flipped back into the Victim role again.

LEARNED HELPLESSNESS

Learned helplessness is a lifelong pattern of victimization in which people learn how to get their needs met through manipulation. Humans with learned helplessness patterns are unable to respond to opportunities or situations that contain positive rewards. It's like an exercise in opposites — pain and suffering are good, and joy and happiness are bad.

Learned helplessness is a common cause of clinical depression in people who believe they have no control over the outcomes of their life situations. They see no possibility of changing things, and they give up and become Victims.

The key to resolving patterns of learned helplessness is to increase personal awareness through education. It's not possible to just empower people who struggle with learned helplessness. They also require a process of unlearning or forgetting, and then learning again in a new fashion.

Learned helplessness is a belief — a twisted belief. The twisted core belief is that *"no matter what I do, nothing will change. My condition or situation is hopeless and I am helpless to change it."*

How can you overcome learned helplessness? How is it possible to change your core beliefs if you aren't really aware of them? The first step is recognizing how twisted beliefs are controlling one's life circumstances. These twisted beliefs keep you stuck. It takes time to change twisted negative beliefs.

The biggest help you can offer others is challenging their negative or twisted belief that helplessness is their only option. People can learn new and more hopeful beliefs about themselves, other people and the world around them. This process requires patience and persistence.

Let's say, for example, your learned helplessness is about communicating with the opposite sex. In this case, the twisted belief about the helplessness can be formulated like this: *"I am not able to get women to like me."* This twisted belief causes the helplessness.

To overcome learned helplessness, people need support in exposing themselves to the same situation again and again, even though it produces anxiety. They need help developing positive beliefs that are learned through effective action.

We've found support groups are an extremely effective mechanism for helping people work through learned helplessness and Victim Consciousness issues. There is something about the power of the group that helps people break through their internal barriers and change their behaviors. The role-modeling aspect in this process is extremely important and transformative.

POWER AND POWERLESSNESS IN THE DRAMA TRIANGLE

Those who see themselves as special, powerful, omnipotent and entitled to dominate others typically play the Persecutor role. They may appear powerful on the outside, but inside they often feel weak and powerless. They just use narcissistic behavior and the Persecutor role to cover up their fears of failure and their desire to also be a Victim. Then they can get their needs met without having to give anything in return.

Persecutors are often envious and jealous of Victims because they see how they get the kind special treatment that Persecutors want. They typically bully others into giving them what they need.

While their unconscious desire is to become a Victim, Persecutors are usually ashamed to be seen as vulnerable and needy. Persecutor types are also trapped in their role because they must manipulate others to get special treatment. It is a similar kind of learned helplessness, just the flip side of the same coin.

Drama Triangle dynamics typically include these twisted beliefs:

- The stronger always dominates the weaker.
- I end up losing whenever I have a conflict.
- People always take advantage of me.
- I believe there isn't enough of what I need available.
- I cannot be direct about what I think or feel.
- It is important to keep secrets in order to feel safe.
- In any conflict someone has to win and someone has to lose.
- I need to suppress my authentic feelings and emotions.
- I use power plays to intimidate others so that I can get my needs met.

Some common power plays are:

- Shaming others
- Escalation ("rage-aholic" behavior)
- Sandbagging (dragging in old issues)
- Asking why instead of how
- Blaming others
- Pulling rank
- Labeling and name-calling
- Leaving in the middle of a conflict
- Avoiding responsibility for a conflict
- Playing the martyr
- Using money or sex to control others.

It can be difficult to change the power balance in Drama Triangle games because much of the industrialized world operates on this dominator/dominated game model. People who are highly committed to changing this cultural system risk being attacked and viewed as unpatriotic, strange or weird.

We recommend that you change your own dominator/ dominated patterns before you attempt to work as change agents in groups or larger systems such as corporations and governments. Otherwise, there's a high probability that you'll get caught up in Drama Triangle dynamics that force you to reveal your personal wounds on a very large stage where you encounter a lot savvy game-players.

In order to effectively help large systems move into healthier social interactions, change agents need to have developed the following personal beliefs:

- I believe there are abundant opportunities to get my needs met, if I am willing to ask directly for what I want or need.
- I believe in the rule of law that protects me and others from unfair treatment.
- I believe social systems operate best when they are constructed to share power.
- I can negotiate with others if I need their help in getting my needs met.
- I believe in using direct lines of communication in my dealings with others.
- I believe in the open expression of feelings, when appropriate.
- I use cooperative, win-win approaches when resolving conflicts.
- I have a commitment to tell the truth and to seek intimacy.
- I show respect for the boundaries of others.

CHAPTER SIX

THE INTERNAL DRAMA TRIANGLE

"Those who can get you to believe absurdities,
can get you to perform atrocities."

—*Voltaire*

We can act out the Drama Triangle internally through dialogue between our internal parts. We can shift between internal roles as quickly as we do out in the world. The inner parts of our psyche can take on the P, V & R roles, and we can literally spend hours staging inner theater.

A common place where you play out your inner theatre is through addictions. You can use your judging parental part to act out the Persecutor role and blast your inner child part for being stupid, lazy or incompetent.

When your inner child/Victim part collapses and becomes depressed, your Rescuer part heads for its favorite addiction to soothe your sad child. Your inner Rescuer justifies this action while you are using it to minimize and to blame others for your problem. You feel a little better temporarily, but it doesn't last, so you blast your Rescuer for being addicted, and the game starts all over.

Internally or externally, you can initiate the game from any of the three Triangle roles. Externally, it often starts with the Victim person fishing for a Rescue. The Victim might say, "I don't have enough money to pay my rent." There is no request for assistance, only a pause waiting for a Rescuer to jump in and offer help.

The Victim may try this with a number of people, but usually calculates the most likely place to find a Rescuer. If no one bites, the Victim can shift to the Persecutor role and try to blame someone for not Rescuing. The Victim can say, "It's your fault that I got my self in this pickle. Didn't you see I needed help?," or something similar to try to make the Rescuer feel guilty.

Because most people internalize their parents as actors in their drama, it's really easy to play this same game inside your head. It truly becomes an inner Mind Game!

A friend shared a recent example of his internal drama Triangle. He decided to go on a vegetarian diet because he was gaining weight — self-Rescuing. For the first several days he felt less energy and got increasingly more irritable. Then he began to doubt the value of the diet, and got angry at himself for starting this "dumb diet" — self-Persecuting.

Finally, he jumped in his car and drove to a hot dog stand where he ate three hot dogs and drank a Coke. Then he got sick and felt like a Victim because his diet didn't allow him to lose weight. So he beat up himself for not being able to follow through with his diet plan. This was the final payoff: He could then be a helpless Victim who couldn't take care of himself.

THE DRAMA TRIANGLE AND VICTIM CONSCIOUSNESS

Perhaps you noticed in the earlier family Drama Triangle example that none of your family members asked directly for what they wanted or needed. Instead, each person complained, threatened, blamed and manipulated others in order to avoid accountability for their part of the problem. This kind of indirect communication perpetuates the game, allowing everyone to feel justified in venting repressed emotions.

Drama Triangle dynamics provide Persecutors with a payoff, a justifiable reason for releasing pent-up emotions from the past. Present-time situations that contain just the right cues will also trigger the release of unprocessed emotions from past conflicts. When this happens, people have difficulty believing that the intensity of their emotions is *not* related to what's happening in the here-and-now.

In fact, the dynamics of the Drama Triangle actually prevent people from connecting the dots between past traumas and emotions and present events and emotions. The dynamics encourage them to blame others for stirring up old, repressed feelings rather than to look inward and ask, "Why am I having such a strong reaction?"

While the Drama Triangle and Victim Consciousness are embedded in the fabric of our societal structures, they are learned first in your family of origin. Very few adults have completed their psychological birth on schedule and are emotionally mature. Psychological birth happens when you develop a strong internal sense of who you are: Your Self. This can begin to happen as early as three years of age, and it allows you to operate on internal power.

If you have not developed a strong sense of self, you will continue to play out co-dependent and counter-dependent games in your adult relationships in an attempt to get your needs met. This means that you will have split or polarized thinking, act out patterns of victimization, and unconsciously play Drama Triangle games.

We see Victim Consciousness as both a developmental issue and an evolutionary issue. When you personally have completed the important developmental tasks of individuation — bonding, separation, autonomy, and mastery and cooperation — you naturally move out of Victim Consciousness. You become self-directed rather than other-directed.

Few of us were able to complete the individuation process at the appropriate time, and therefore it is challenging to break free of Victim Consciousness as an adult. Later in this book we'll share tools that you can use to complete your individuation process and become self-directed, no matter what your age.

Only when enough individuals have become self-directed can the human species truly move forward in its evolution. For the human race to evolve, we each must complete the essential developmental processes of early childhood, even if we have to do it as adults. Then we can break free of Victim Consciousness.

CHAPTER SEVEN

RELIGIOUS BELIEFS THAT TRAP US IN THE DRAMA TRIANGLE & VICTIM CONSCIOUSNESS

"We must take sides. Neutrality helps the oppressor, never the victim. Silence encourages the tormentor, never the tormented."

—Elie Wiesel

Almost all denominations of Christianity believe in the concept of Original Sin. The exceptions are the Orthodox Churches — the so-called Restoration Movement Churches such as the Church of Christ and the Disciples of Christ, and the Church of Latter Day Saints. Currently, about 136 million Christian church members belong to churches that believe in the doctrine of Original Sin. You may be surprised to find that this concept was not part of early Christianity.

A Catholic monk, Augustine of Hippo, is said to have invented the concept of Original Sin in the 5th century A.D. It was mostly forgotten after that until it was re-introduced by Anselm in the 11th century. Eventually it found its way into medieval philosophy. From there, it became an accepted belief in the Roman Catholic Church, and was eventually also adopted by the Protestants.

The concept of Original Sin is completely unknown in Judaism. It is also unknown among the indigenous Christian churches of Greece, the Balkans, Africa, Eastern Europe, Russia, and the Muslim faith in the Middle East, Iraq, Iran and India.

According to Islam, every one is born clean. That is why they believe every child will go to heaven no matter whether being born to the best or worst family. The Prophet Muhammad said, "He who makes a pilgrimage to Mecca with sincerity will return like the day he was born" — clean of any sin.

Islam also does not even believe in sin by derivation. This means that sin is not transferable and therefore is limited to the person who committed it. A child does not inherit the sins of the father or mother. The Quran says in the 2nd chapter (*surat al Baqara*) that after Adam and Eve sinned, God taught them how to repent, they did, and he forgave them. This is where the issue of the Original Sin ended for Islam.

ORIGINAL SIN IS BASED ON BIBLICAL MISINTERPRETATION

The concept of Original Sin is based on a Biblical misinterpretation of Romans 5:12. This passage says that sin began when Adam disobeyed God, and the result was his spiritual death or separation from God. The verse goes on to state that everyone since this time was born into sin.

It does not say, however, that Christians inherited their sin from Adam. This assumption gradually found its way into Biblical text. In John 3:7 Jesus said, "Flesh gives birth to flesh, but the Spirit gives birth to spirit." In other words, when we are born, we are flesh, not spirit.

Without a spiritual connection to God, we follow the impulses of our bodies. We do what feels good. There is nothing inherently sinful about our emotions or our bodily pleasures. Unfortunately, sin became defined as a commitment to what pleases and is pleasurable without regard to what others have decided is God's will.

Since we begin at birth to do what comes naturally, fulfilling our physical needs, we learn to live for our own pleasure. As we grow and develop a conscience, we become aware of right and wrong, and we recognize that others have needs and rights as well. This is how we become aware there is a higher purpose beyond seeking self-fulfillment.

James 2:14 – 15 states, "Each one is tempted when, by his own desire, he is dragged away and enticed. Then, after desire has conceived, it gives birth to sin; and sin, when it is full-grown, gives birth to death."

The other source said to validate this doctrine comes from Psalm 51:5. "Behold, I was shapen in iniquity, and in sin did my mother conceive me." This statement is about David's conception, and relates to his mother being defined as a sinner. But it does not say he was born a sinner. That interpretation was added later.

WHY HAS ORIGINAL SIN PERSISTED SO LONG?

Why has this twisted belief continued to influence our thinking? Likely it's because it serves as a powerful tool for controlling the Christian masses. Christian churches promise believers salvation and redemption from their Original Sin if they are willing to follow religious doctrine, contribute money to the church, and then expect the church to rescue them from their sins.

If believers follow the very lofty standards set up by the Church, which only a perfect person could do, their soul will be saved and they will have everlasting life. Otherwise, they'll burn in hell for eternity.

This twisted religious belief makes people dependent on the approval of church leaders, and they have to follow what others say is true. By comparing themselves to God or Jesus — "What would Jesus do?" —people fall short and are found wanting or sinful. This is a foolproof mechanism for trapping the masses in Victim Consciousness.

If you believe in Original Sin, you've given someone else the power to define and measure your worth. You are dependent on the hoops they want you to jump through to be saved from eternal damnation and to be granted everlasting life. This trap is very difficult to escape and supports a lifetime of Victim Consciousness and dependency on the church for your well-being.

WHAT IS THE SAVIOR COMPLEX?

The cornerstone of Christianity is the belief that if you confess your sins and are forgiven by the church leaders, you will have eternal life. This belief takes the Persecutor/Victim bond to the next level. When we add the role of the divine Rescuer to the mix, the Drama Triangle trap is set. This trap is known as the Savior Complex. There are three parts to this complex set of twisted beliefs:

1. You cannot help but sin because that is your very nature. Since you have no control over your sinful behavior, you can only be victimized by it.
2. It is religious Persecutors' job to remind you of how you have sinned. They are in charge of deciding whether you have jumped through the hoops they've set for you and whether you are worthy of being saved.
3. Jesus Christ died for our sins. He and the church leaders (Rescuers), as his representatives, can save you from eternal damnation.

Essential to this Christian dynamic is a belief that you must strive to be like Jesus, which of course sets you up for failure. Sinners are expected to emulate this unattainable model of perfection. There is no way out of this trap once you buy in.

The Savior Complex gives the church leaders total power over your life and allows them to dominate and control — Persecute — people. It also inflicts enormous suffering in life. In order to be saved, you first must admit to being a sinner — a Victim. If you repent, then you are forgiven and will be saved — Rescued.

You certainly don't want to be spiritually overlooked and told your sins aren't big enough to deserve the Church's attention. All of this sets up competition for being seen as the biggest sinner (Victim). And like the Persecutor/Victim bond, your sinful nature is the cause of your suffering. The greater the suffering, the better your chance of being saved.

This sinner attitude encourages the church to inflict suffering on people. Then the church can blame people for their suffering and sinful nature — and then invite them to be saved, if they repent and give up their sinful ways. What a deal!

Belief in the Savior Complex contains an unspoken permission to victimize and inflict suffering on anyone the church declares a heretic or a nonbeliever. It was exactly this twisted justification that caused the Roman Catholic Church to commit genocide against the Pagans and Gnostics in Europe. It is also the same justification used by early Americans in the New World to commit genocide on the native populations and plunder their riches. Similarly, the Nazis used a version of this belief to justify their persecution of the Jews.

CHRISTIANITY'S TWISTED BELIEFS

Early Christians created a set of twisted beliefs to anchor the Savior Complex in people's minds. This complex, which evolved over the centuries, is still at the core of Christianity. In order to accept the Savior Complex, you must believe:

- There is a heaven and a hell.
- If you do not confess your sins and are not saved, you will burn in hell for eternity.
- You must worship a God in Heaven, somewhere up in the sky.
- You must have faith in and believe in the existence of an unknowable off-planet God.

- Jesus, the Son of God, died on the cross to redeem you of your sins.
- If you are saved, you will not die, but live forever in a place called Heaven.
- In order to be saved, you must accept that you were born a sinner (Original Sin) and you will always be a sinner, even if your sins are forgiven.
- You must be told what is a sin and what is not by people who claim to be experts on these matters, because you aren't able to figure it out for yourself.
- You must be part of an organized religion and expect the clergy of some church to decide whether you have sinned.
- Because of your sinful nature, you need the church and its clergy to help you keep from sinning and/or to forgive you when you sin.
- If you follow your natural urges, experience pleasure and commit sins, you're at risk of eternal damnation.
- In order to determine whether or not you are becoming a True Christian, you must compare yourself to Jesus and be able to accomplish what he was supposedly able to do.
- Otherwise you are not a good Christian but a lowly sinner.

The Savior Complex is a program that leads you away from trusting yourself and towards trusting religious or other external authorities to determine your goodness as a person. This is a great formula for creating a False Self that says and does what will please others, including Jesus and God. You will not be able to create an authentic Self. No, you'll operate out of a False Self that the church accepts. Doing this, however, also absolves you from taking responsibility for your life.

The church acts as a parent, and you fall into the trap of being a child and believing the church knows more about what is good for you than you do. This is a sure formula for victimhood and learned helplessness. When you give away your power to create your authentic self, it is very hard to get it back again.

When humanity is trapped in Victim Consciousness, it is powerless to resist the violence that the church has used regularly over the centuries. John Lash says in his book, *Not In His Image* (2009), "*In the final balance the people who commit and promote violence and murder in the expression of religious beliefs may be a minute fraction of the faithful, but they are the ones who determine the course of events, shape history, affect society, and threaten the biosphere.*" (p. 239)

Lash concludes, *"History shows that the religious beliefs attached to (the) salvation narrative have consistently been used to legitimize violence, rape, genocide, and destruction of the natural world."* (p. 238)

The impact of twisted political, religious, and spiritual beliefs on our daily lives is enormous and keeps us trapped in Victim Consciousness. Every time we encounter people with twisted religious and spiritual beliefs, it has a negative impact on us.

The influence of these twisted beliefs is so prevalent, we're virtually unaware of the negative impact it has on us. It keeps us trapped in religious Victim Consciousness. In order to make sure twisted beliefs are not keeping you trapped, we encourage you to examine your own religious beliefs for twists and clear them. In the second part of this book we show you how to do this.

THE TWISTED GOLDEN RULE

John Lash points out an important twist in the Christian belief of the Golden Rule. Jesus supposedly uttered this rule when asked, *"Which is the first commandment of all?"* His answer was reported to be, *"Do unto others as you would have them do unto you."*

A closer look historically and linguistically, however, shows that this expression comes from an earlier saying by the Jewish Rabbi Hillel, which the early Christian Church altered so that it would better serve its agenda.

Hillel's rule stated, *"Do not do unto others that which is hateful unto thee."* Lash astutely points out that Hillel's statement avoids the idea of reward and punishment. The twist in the Christian version focuses on what we want from others rather than what we don't want. On the surface this doesn't seem like a big deal.

Lash points out, however, that the Christian Golden Rule contains an expectation that if I do something for others, I will get something of equal value in return. This causes people to focus on the behavior of others so that they can get something back from them, and that these people are now obligated to give something in return. This kind of twist encourages people to manipulate each other to get what they each want rather than ask for it directly.

The second twist in the Golden Rule that Lash identifies is the difference between doing onto others vs. not doing unto others. The latter talks about how to avoid doing things and keeps the focus inward on your own needs. The former, however, keeps you focused outward on the needs of others.

Focusing on the needs of others instead on your own needs describes classic codependent behaviors.

How does this Need/Obligate System work in practice? Here's an example. If I want my boss to give me a new car, I would have to first purchase one for him. This twist is important because it states that if you want a reward, you have to reward someone else, who is then obligated to give you something in return of equal value.

As Lash states, *"You are obligated to treat others in whatever way that you might want them to treat you."* (p. 238) This is the central dynamic in the Need/Obligate System, which we describe in the next chapter.

NOTES

1   Lash, J. (2006). *Not in his image. Chelsea Green Publishing: White River Junction, VT. p. 254.*

CHAPTER EIGHT

THE NEED/OBLIGATE SYSTEM
AND THE DRAMA TRIANGLE

*"If right and left are competing to be the biggest
victim, who is competing to be the government?"*

—*David Frum*

The Need/Obligate System is a variation of the Drama Triangle. It's a component of the "good old boy" and "good old girl" networks found in organizations and corporations. Here is how it works:

1. Someone does something for you without first asking you.
2. They expect you to be grateful for what they've done for you.
3. You return their favor without their having to ask for it.

The implicit agreement, never spoken, is that "I did this favor for you, and now you are obligated to return it." This means you've been Rescued and are now obligated to Rescue in return. In this game, you must figure out what this other person needs and give it without their having to ask for it. That's why it's called the Need/Obligate System.

If you don't repay the other person's favor in just the right way, you run the risk of being Persecuted. Your failure permits them to get angry about your lack of thoughtfulness. If you accept the person's Rescue and don't repay their favor, the Rescuer feels cheated and becomes a Victim. This game is so prevalent in organizations that it permeates their day-to-day operations. It's also the source of most organizational conflicts, gossip and rumors.

The Need/Obligate System trains you to do things for others without their having to ask. This is also the defining quality of all co-dependent interactions and the primary reason people use Drama Triangle dynamics to get their needs met.

DISORGANIZED ATTACHMENT AND THE NEED/OBLIGATE SYSTEM

Developmental trauma and disorganized attachment are the primary causes of the Need/Obligate System. Developmental trauma, by our definition, is the result of disorganized attachment (DA) and disturbed mother-child dynamics during the first year of life.

By age six, children with DA typically develop one of three common behavior patterns. These patterns involve "parentizing," in which the child gives up his or her needs and focuses on providing either physical or emotional support to the mother or primary attachment figure. The purpose of this "reversal process" is to support the mother so that she becomes more capable of caring for the child.

The three common behavior patterns in six-year-olds with the DA style are "The Little General," "The Solicitous Caregiver" and "The Lost Child." We use these names because they capture the heart of children's valiant efforts to provide support for their mother and father so that he/she can take care of them.

The Little General is directive, telling the mother what to do and when and how to do it. This child provides physical organization in the environment around the mother and becomes quite proficient as a manager for the mother's world. Unfortunately, neither the mother nor the Little General ever focuses on identifying or meeting the child's needs. The child may become quite effective and efficient in organizing the lives of others, but have virtually no skills or understanding about how to organize their own life. These people are the Persecutors in the Drama Triangle.

The Solicitous Caregiver provides emotional support for the mother, often being the peacemaker and smoothing out any upsets or conflicts in the environment. These children are often empathic and overly sensitive, and become emotionally hypervigilant to the mother's needs. These become the Rescuers in the Drama Triangle.

The Lost Child lacks enough internal resources to organize the physical or emotional environment around the mother. This child is often chronically dissociated and not mentally or emotionally present. Much of the time they are waiting for someone to make contact with them in a Rescuing way. These people are the Victims in the Drama Triangle.

People with these three coping patterns become highly skilled in identifying other people's needs but have virtually no skills in understanding or meeting their own. Very early these children learn to be efficient caretakers and rescuers, and they become effective participants in both the Need/Obligate System and the Drama Triangle.

CHARACTERISTICS OF DISORGANIZED ATTACHMENT

There are two hallmark traits of individuals with DA. The first is an inability to self-regulate and self-soothe intense emotions. The second is a lack of self-awareness about their own emotional needs. They are so focused on game playing and meeting the needs of others that they are unable to organize their own lives. Consequently, they struggle to lead self-directed lives, regardless of their intelligence.

Subtle, relational developmental trauma is so pervasive in our global society that it has become virtually invisible. Two of our goals in writing this book are to make the world aware of the effects of this form of chronic relational trauma and to provide tools for healing it so that humanity can evolve.

Most people who seek counseling have Disorganized Attachment and struggle with disorganized and chaotic patterns of behavior. They have limited ability to connect cause with effect, which interferes with their ability to predict the outcomes of their choices. Because the world seems random and unpredictable, much of their life operates through trial and error. Logic is a foreign language, which makes planning and strategic thinking very difficult.

The most needed skill for those with Disorganized Attachment is the ability to connect childhood events and experiences to their adult conflicts, issues and problems. This is the primary goal for helping people create a coherent life narrative. It helps people develop cause-and-effect thinking and use it in their lives. It also help people exit the Drama Triangle.

POLITICS AND THE NEED/OBLIGATE SYSTEM

All Washington lobbyists and politicians use the Need/Obligate system. A lobbyist approaches a member of Congress, for example, and donates a sum of money to their campaign fund without the Congressperson ever asking directly for it. Then the politician is obligated to vote a certain way on legislation related to the lobbyist's interests.

Nothing is ever transacted directly or written down. The members of Congress know that if they do not vote the way this lobbyist wishes, it will be the end of the campaign contributions from that source.

We believe the best way you can protect yourself from the Need-Obligate and other dysfunctional, codependent Drama Triangle games is to know thyself very well. The better you understand yourself, the more able you'll be to avoid manipulation and entanglements.

PART TWO

HOW TO BREAK FREE OF
THE DRAMA TRIANGLE

CHAPTER NINE

STEPS IN BREAKING FREE OF
THE DRAMA TRIANGLE

"Definition of a victim: a person to whom life happens."

—*Peter McWilliams*

Even though Drama Triangle dynamics seem benign, they aren't. They keep you stuck feeling powerless and helpless in Victim Consciousness, unable to get your needs met directly. They also block the completion of your psychological birth and the development of your full identity, and keep you functioning as an adult child.

Here are the five steps we've identified for breaking free of the Drama Triangle. We describe these in more detail in the remainder of this chapter.

1. Commit to getting your needs met by asking directly for what you want and need. This means giving up your Victim behaviors and exiting Victim Consciousness.
2. Refuse to rescue other people. Don't do anything for anyone else unless they have asked you to do it or you get their permission to do it.
3. Learn to recognize and reclaim your projections. This involves looking at your judgments of others to see if they might represent things you don't like about yourself.
4. Recognize and heal your developmental traumas. Notice the things that trigger you and cause a reaction that is greater than the situation called for. This is an indication of an unhealed trauma.
5. Learn to express your thoughts and feelings authentically in the moment rather than saving them up and then dumping them. When you don't express your feelings at the time you first feel them, they tend to come out more strongly and less authentically.

When you are able to do these five things, you will eliminate the Drama Triangle from your life. You will successfully move out of Victim Consciousness, and you will be free of the only game in town.

ASKING DIRECTLY FOR WHAT YOU WANT

In order to break free of Victim Consciousness, you must take charge of meeting your own needs. You must be willing to ask for what you want or need 100% of the time. This doesn't mean that you will actually have to ask for everything that you want and need, only that you are willing to do this.

You'll know that you have mastered being direct when you can ask for what you want in such a way that others are delighted to give it to you. If this isn't happening, you're probably still using co-dependent and/or counter-dependent transactions.

Asking for what you want and need helps you separate emotionally and psychologically from those in your close circle of friends and family. This skill will also help you become less dependent on collective consciousness and the group mind. You will have less concern about what other people think of you and more concern about following your own guidance.

This is not easy, as the power of group thinking is very strong. It takes a great deal of determination and the focused use of your intention to follow your own internal guidance and to act from your personal power.

This is not necessarily bad, because pushing against this resistance can help activate and expand your sense of strength. In other words, you can use the power of the group mind as a kind of negative ally to test your abilities to be clear, direct and conscious, and to follow your inner guidance even when others disapprove.

Individuating means learning to trust your inner knowing and to take full responsibility for creating the experiences of your life. No longer can you blame what is happening to you on others, bad luck, or anything else. Becoming personally responsible for your life is a big part of learning to break free of Victim Consciousness.

HOW TO BREAK FREE OF VICTIM CONSCIOUSNESS

The process of breaking free of Victim Consciousness means identifying family traumas, experiences, beliefs and behavior patterns that keep you trapped in the group mind or matrix. Identifying and healing the effects of trauma, particularly from early childhood, is a big part of this process.

This trauma makes you vulnerable to the Drama Triangle and traps you in Victim Consciousness. Here is a simple exercise that will help you identify childhood trauma.

SELF-AWARENESS EXERCISE: THE TWO LISTS

Directions: Use this exercise to identify past experiences that make you vulnerable to Drama Triangle and Victim Consciousness. On a blank sheet of paper make a chart like the one below, filling in the blanks using the directions below.

WHAT I WANTED & DIDN'T GET	WHAT I WANTED & DIDN'T GET
MOTHER	*FATHER*
WHAT I GOT & DIDN'T WANT	WHAT I GOT & DIDN'T WANT
MOTHER	*FATHER*

1. In the top rows, list of all the things that you wish your mother and father had done for you or said to you while you were growing up. These are things you believe would have made your adult life easier had you gotten them. These are the things you feel may have held you back. Examples: "I wish she had told me directly that she loved me" or "I wish he had given me birthday parties and been there to help me celebrate my birthday." Place these items in either the "mother" box in the left column or "father" box in the right column.

2. In the bottom rows, review your childhood to recall things that you wish had not been done or said to you while you were growing up. This list represents the things that hurt or damaged you and adversely affected your adult life in some important way. Examples: "I wish he hadn't humiliated me when I got pregnant in high school" or "I wish she hadn't punished me by calling me names and hitting me." Place these items in the bottom two rows of the "mother" and "father" columns.

INTERPRETATION OF THE TWO LISTS

Row #1: What I wanted that I didn't get. These events caused developmental traumas starting as early as the first year of life. These very early traumas can have negative effects throughout your childhood and later as an adult. They indicate where you experienced early bonding trauma that left

51

you with unmet needs. Typically these events involved unintentional emotional abandonment and neglect.

The items on this list often leave you with an expectation that the only way to get your needs met in your adult relationships is by not asking directly. As a result of such early traumas, you likely doubt that you can ask those close to you for their help in meeting your needs.

You may even find yourself attempting to manipulate or control others in order to get these needs met, while also trying to avoid the feelings related to the initial trauma. Unhealed trauma from early childhood trauma makes you vulnerable to playing out both the Victim and the Rescuer roles on the Drama Triangle.

Rather than being a Victim, use the events you placed in Row #1 as a healing list. Identify where and with whom you can get each need met, and place the names of a person or persons currently in your life who could help you meet these needs.

Perhaps you still feel angry and resentful toward your mother or father, or are fantasizing that they will eventually give you what you need without your initiating it. Or maybe you fear asking for what you want because you might be refused or rejected.

These passive strategies don't work. They just keep you locked in anger, resentment and rejection, and feeling hopeless, helpless and victimized. You can stay stuck in your childhood wounds, or you can take charge of your life and ask directly to get your needs met.

Row #2: What I got that I did not want. This column is related to traumas experienced during the counter-dependent stage of development, ages 1–3. The items on this list are usually related to hurtful and abusive experiences — harmful things that were said or done to you while you were growing up, starting at an early age. These traumas make it difficult to be close to others.

People who exhibit counter-dependent body language often say to themselves, "I have built a wall around me and I'm not going to let you see who I really am. I'm not going to let you get close to me because I don't want to get hurt again." They engage in defensive behaviors that hide their vulnerability.

WORKING WITH THE TWO LISTS

If you have many items listed on Row #2, you likely have erected protective defenses to prevent closeness and vulnerability. This puts you in a bind. You may want to get close to others so that you can get your needs met, but because you fear being hurt again, you're afraid to take the risk.

To break through this, you must clear unhealed trauma from your nervous system. This helps remove the barriers that prevent you from receiving love and support from others. In Chapter Eleven we describe how to do this.

Working with the issues listed in Row #2 often requires using the tool of forgiveness. We define forgiveness a bit unusually. Our version involves giving back or forgiving those things that do not belong to you. This includes other people's beliefs, emotions and definitions of who you are. It also involves reclaiming any parts of yourself you might have buried or split off, such as your spontaneity, your playfulness, your sense of humor and your beliefs that are congruent with your conscience.

Using our perspective on forgiveness, you can clear resentment and Victim energy from your consciousness. As long as you continue to hold on to anger and resentment toward those who've hurt you in the past, you'll remain stuck in Victim Consciousness and be unable to evolve.

We also use the empty-chair technique to help people clear feelings of fear, anger and resentment. This experiential exercise involves putting an empty chair across from you and imagining that a parent or person with whom you have unresolved issues is seated in it. Then you dialogue with this person about your experiences and issues.

First you ask this person questions. Then you switch chairs and become the other person, answering the questions you have just asked. Use you imagination and intuition to help you respond in the way this person would if they were really truthful with you.

This technique not only creates insight about why this other person did these hurtful things, it often produces compassion, understanding, and the ability to forgive. We've found the empty chair technique to be highly transformative.

If you have a partner, we suggest doing the Two Lists exercise separately and then sharing your answers. Couples often find that speaking the truth about their hidden issues can be both healing and freeing.

The Two Lists can also provide a structure for working cooperatively to get your needs met in an intimate relationship. In the first list you've each identified unmet needs you're hoping can be met in your relationship. Sharing your Two Lists with each other can help you negotiate directly to meet those childhood needs.

The items on the second list show where you are holding anger and resentment. Your partner can encourage you to release your fear, anger and resentment in a safe and loving environment. We recommend anger release techniques involving vigorous activity, such as beating on an old beanbag chair with a tennis racquet, hammering, pounding pillows or other items, running, and screaming in your closed car.

It is likely that you, like most people, experienced trauma during both the co-dependent and counter-dependent stages of development. It is easy to gauge how much trauma you experienced during this period by looking at which of your two lists is longer or seems to have more emotional charge. Once you have identified the sources of your traumas, it is possible to clear them from your nervous system using the tools in Chapter 11.

HOW TO RECOGNIZE A RESCUE

We each have a favorite role for entering the Drama Triangle, which we learned in our family of origin. Parentized children or children who function as Solicitous Caregivers typically enter the Drama Triangle from the Rescuer role. This is because they've been conditioned to be people-pleasing caretakers.

Parentized children who function as Little Generals like to avoid conflict, to avoid drama, to have the answers, to feel important, and to be in charge. They often become teachers, ministers, doctors or nurses, working in the helping or healing professions. They also are particularly susceptible to entering the Drama Triangle through the Rescuer role.

Here's a list of the most common ways people enter the Drama Triangle through the Rescuer role:

- Do something for someone that you really don't want to do
- Try to meet other people's needs without being asked.
- Consistently do more than your fair share of the work in a helping situation
- Feel so uncomfortable with receiving that you find it necessary
- Have relationships with others in which you can only give and not receive

- Try to fix other people's feelings or talk them out of their feelings
- Speak up for other people instead of letting them speak for themselves
- Refuse to ask for what you need and attend only to the needs of others
- Feel rejected when your help is graciously refused
- Try to help others without an explicit contract. This does not include acts of kindness and compassion where help is legitimately needed.

Counselors and other professional helpers can easily become engaged in the Drama Triangle with their clients and can ultimately traumatize their clients, because counselors tend to attract clients with similar issues to their own. The counselor's own hidden and unhealed traumas can provoke mutual or interlocking counselor-client drama. Without training and awareness, it's easy for counselors and clients to get caught up in this kind of painful dynamic.

This professional pitfall is known in the counseling profession as countertransference. It is critical that professional helpers work diligently to clear their own unhealed childhood traumas and be aware of what makes them vulnerable to being sucked onto the Drama Triangle.

People who were repeatedly rescued in their families, particularly by their parents, older parentized siblings, or grandparents, typically enter the Drama Triangle through the Victim role. They use conflict and drama to manipulate others into taking care of them and meeting their needs without their having to ask directly for this caretaking.

Those who were abused as children often enter the Drama Triangle through the Persecutor role, as it provides them with a way to express their pent up childhood emotions and to pass on their abuse through a vicious cycle of cruelty. They find someone who is a bigger Victim with whom they act out their desire for revenge.

CHAPTER TEN

HOW TO RECOGNIZE WHEN YOU ARE PROJECTING

"Don't Take Anything Personally.
Nothing others do is because of you.
What others say and do is a projection
of their own reality, their own dream.
When you are immune to the opinions and actions of others,
you won't be the victim of needless suffering."

—Miguel Don Ruiz

Our world is filled with people who project their hidden parts on others. It is the most common way people avoid looking at the parts of themselves they do not like or accept. They project these unwanted qualities unto others. They see in others what they refuse to see in themselves.

Most people don't recognize when they are projecting — of course not! They are totally focused on what another person is saying or doing that is making them feel upset. The first sign of an active projection is the appearance of the pointy finger, usually accompanied by a shaming and/or blaming comment that begins with the word "you."

When they are projecting, people often want someone to stop whatever they are saying or doing. They say things like, "Would you please stop chewing your gum so loud! You are making me angry!"

Projections also typically involve judgments about other people — how they look, how they behave, what they believe, or what they are doing or saying. Judging others helps us avoid seeing parts of ourselves that either we or someone else dislikes.

For example, if bossy people irritate and trigger you because they take over or dominate people, you have a judgment about "bossy people." You may also have control issues.

The bossy person is just doing what they do. Your reaction to their bossiness is all about you. Either you wish you could be bossy (envy), you're too bossy yourself (a projection), or you have unprocessed trauma from exposure to bossy people (anger and resentment).

Sometimes our judgments show up as unclassified emotions. We're uncomfortable and want the other person to change or stop their behavior. Instead of going inside and asking, "Why am I having this reaction to what X is doing?," we blame our emotional overreaction on the other person.

A variation of this is saying to someone, "You make me feel angry!" No one makes us feel anything. We feel the way we feel because of our inner experiences and the way we interact with the world. Taking responsibility for our emotions and emotional reactions is a critical part of getting off the Drama Triangle.

When we project, we almost always personalize the other person's behavior. We see what they are doing as a personal insult and that they are doing it to us just to irritate us.

In truth, people do what they do for their own reasons. They don't sit around thinking to themselves, "Hmmmm, wonder what I could do to bug John or make him upset?" No, the other person is in their own world and trying to cope with their own inner demons. You know you or someone else is projecting when:

- You have a fifty-cent reaction to a ten-cent event
- You want someone to stop saying or doing something because it brings up unwanted feelings and you feel uncomfortable
- You blame your unwanted feelings on other people
- You say, "You made me feel ____!"
- You personalize what other people do and say, believing they are doing it to deliberately hurt you or upset you.

Once you understand how projections operate, it's important to recognize when you are using them. Use the self-inventory below to help you discover more about how you use projections.

PROJECTIONS SELF-INVENTORY

On a scale of 1 to 4, indicate how frequently these beliefs influence how you think about yourself and others.

Key: 1 = Hardly Ever; 2 = Sometimes; 3 = Frequently; 4 = Almost Always

_____ 1.   My reactions to conflicts are far greater than they should be.

_____ 2.   When I am in conflict, I have feelings that remind me of how I felt in past conflict situations.

_____ 3.   In a conflict situation, I find myself focusing on what the other person is saying or doing.

_____ 4.   I find myself using loaded words like *always* or *never* to describe conflict I have with another person.

_____ 5.   I see in others positive qualities I can't see in myself.

_____ 6.   I see in others negative qualities I have trouble accepting in myself.

_____ 7.   I have trouble admitting a mistake. Instead, I immediately point out something that someone else did or said, and blame them for the mistake.

_____ 8.   I space out when someone tells me something I don't want to hear.

_____ 9.   When I know someone doesn't like me, I avoid them like the plague.

_____ 10. I find myself making moral judgments about the character or behavior of people I don't like.

_____   **TOTAL SCORE**

Interpretation of scores:

10 – 20 = Little evidence of projections.

21 – 30 = Some evidence of projections.

31 – 40 = Strong evidence of projections.

HOW TO RECLAIM YOUR PROJECTIONS

You may have spent the first twenty or more years of your life defending yourself against persecution attacks during Drama Triangle games. You probably protected vital parts of your Self by splitting them off and putting them into a shame bag.

If you'd had your normal narcissistic needs met as a child, you would not need to use projections to defend against attacks. At some point, you can understand what you do and begin reclaiming your split-off parts.

Barry shares an experience in learning about projections. I can remember as an adult writing all the silly things that I was told while I was growing up that I shouldn't do or say, such as, *"Don't talk with your mouth full. You know, if your mouth is full you usually can't talk anyway. "What will the neighbors think?"* I always wanted to go over and knock on their door and ask them what they thought of my behavior, but I never did. I was afraid they knew more about me than I was aware of.

The other thing I heard was, *"Be sure to wear clean underwear in case you get hurt and have to go to the hospital."* Well, I do still wear clean underwear every day, but not because I'm afraid of getting injured.

These examples taught me the power of projection messages. Other family messages were not so benign. My parents and grandparents projected onto me their fear about the world not being a safe place. They told me, *"Be careful when you cross the street, because you might get hit by a car and get killed,"* and, *"Be careful when you go swimming, you might drown."* Their messages seemed to have dire consequences attached to them, which for some time really influenced and even controlled me.

As a child, I was very cautious about taking risks out in the world. I never fully developed my own internal safety parent, so I tried to play it safe in everything I did. Not much fun. Another projection message, which had long-term effects on me, was, *"Don't ask so many questions. Be a good boy. Your parents have enough trouble of their own without you causing them more."* This message from my grandmother really crimped my ability to share my feelings with people for fear of burdening them."

A PROCESS FOR IDENTIFYING AND RECLAIMING PROJECTIONS

Robert Bly, poet, author and wisdom-keeper, describes a five-stage process for reclaiming projections. The first four stages mostly involve trying to make projections work.

Stage One: You're unaware and don't realize you're projecting.

Stage Two: You realize that you're projecting but don't know what to do about it. For example, your spouse isn't always a tyrant or an angry bitch, and sometimes acts lovingly toward you and wants to be close.

What can you do in situations when it is hard not to see the other person as bad or uncaring? Bly says this dilemma may be frightening to you because it brings up your old fears and insecurities. You may try to provoke or manipulate your partner back into the negative role you want them to play out.

In Stage Two, couples sometimes try to solve their dilemma by having children. Parents can project the unacceptable parts of themselves onto their kids, who can't fight back. Children are always taking risks and trying to be themselves, so they make great targets for projections.

Stage Three: Things break down in your relationships because of your projections, and you use moral rightness to justify your actions. Parents may claim they are doing something for your own good when they punish you severely. The message is, "Don't question my authority, I am right."

If your family is religious, they may even invoke a parental God: "*God will punish you if you don't behave or listen to me.*" You may find yourself making moral judgments about what other people or groups are doing, such as, "*The President is an idiot and a warmonger.*"

Stage Four: You let down your guard briefly enough to recognize what you are doing. You may see that you are losing relationships because of your projections. This may cause you to take inventory of your problems and decide to change your life. You also may get into therapy or join a support group and begin connecting the dots to take responsibility for your problems.

Stage Five: The task here is to integrate your Shadow. This means facing every part of yourself that you have split off or pushed onto others. You must chew up, swallow and digest all the parts of yourself that you dislike until you can accept them. By reintegrating these split-off parts, you can access deeper feelings, be more passionate and compassionate about life, and become more spontaneous, health conscious and spiritual.

According to Bly, people who have eaten their Shadow tend to *Be* more than *Do*, and they can express grief more than anger. They often find they have much more energy, need less sleep, and are more wise and discerning in their decisions.

Once you've reclaimed your Shadow, central casting will no longer send people to annoy or provoke you. Until you integrate your unclaimed projections and Shadow parts, you will attract difficult people into your life.

A GROUP PROCESS FOR CLEARING JUDGMENTS AND PROJECTIONS

Some men's support groups use a specific process to help members clear any judgments or projections they have toward another group member. The purpose is to clear any barriers that keep you from being fully present, feeling safe, or be willing to open up and go deeper in your relationship.

The process looks like this:

1. A member indicates he wishes to do a clearing with another group member. The two people stand or sit face-to-face in the center of the group, holding eye contact. Each has a hand on a staff or walking stick with the clearer's hand below the clearee's hand.

2. The person who is the object of the projections or judgments cannot reply during this process. He has to listen silently, putting up a heart shield to protect himself from any negative energy. He can ask for support from other group members, specifying what kind of support he wants. For instance, it may involve asking another group member to stand behind him with hands on their shoulders.

3. The person who is projecting and judging is asked to respond to the question, *"Who is this about?"*

4. This person must reply, *"It is all about me."* If he cannot say this with authenticity, the clearing process is stopped until he can answer truthfully, *"It is all about me."*

4. If he answers *"It is all about me,"* he is asked to answer the next question, *"What are the data?,"* i.e., *"What happened? Just state the facts."* Do not give any feelings, judgments, or adjectives at this point, just an objective description of what was said and done by the other person that triggered a projection or judgment.

5. T. Then he is asked to answer the next question: *"What are you feeling toward this person?"* Be sure to state only feelings, for instance, *"I am*

feeling angry." Do not use non-feeling statements like, "*I am feeling that you lied to me.*"

6. Next, he answers the question, "*Where do you feel these feelings in your body?*" Pay attention to what feelings or sensations you are experiencing in your body, and describe these feelings or sensations. This helps to anchor the feelings in a physical place and prevents you from just talking about your emotions.

7. Then he has to respond to the question, "*What are your judgments?*" At this point, he may express his judgments of the other person crudely, inappropriately, and with no holds barred.

8. He then responds to the question, "*How does this person remind you of yourself? Or remind you of anything about yourself that you don't like?*" If you find these questions difficult to answer, use these ideas to prompt you:

    a. How is he a mirror for you? What do you see in him that you dislike in yourself?

    b. Is he your shadow? How does he remind you of any hidden, re-pressed, or denied feelings or behaviors?

    c. What rules do you have about other people, their conduct, etc? How does this person violate the rules you have for yourself?

    d. Who from your past does this person remind you of? What might be unfinished in your past that is related to your judgments now?

9. The person again is asked to respond to the following question: "*Who is this about?*" He still must be willing to say, "*It is all about me.*" Other-wise, the clearing process is not complete and the person requesting the clearing is asked to do more work on himself until he can reclaim his projections and judgments.

10. Then the person is responds to the question, "Are you willing to with-draw your projections and judgments from this person?" The answer has to be "yes" or again the process breaks down. If the person is not willing to withdraw the projections or judgments, he has to agree to work on this issue before doing any further clearings with this person.

11. Then he is asked to respond to, "What do you want from this person?" Usually the person wants to be forgiven for projecting onto the other person and asks for forgiveness or a hug.

12. Then he is asked, *"Are you complete with this person?"* This person must answer "Yes" or give reasons he does not feel complete.

13. Finally he is asked, *"Do you now feel clear with this person? How do you want to close this clearing process?"*

NOTE: If the person who was the object of projections has resentments come up or feels "picked on" in some way, he is invited to do the same clearing process until he is able to clear these resentments or perceptions and can feel clear with the other person.

CHAPTER ELEVEN

HOW TO HEAL YOUR
DEVELOPMENTAL TRAUMA

"The results of any traumatic experience such as abuse,
can only be resolved by experiencing, articulating
and judging every facet of the original experience
within a process of careful therapeutic disclosure."

—*Alice Miller*

It's important to recognize that your participation in Drama Triangle dynamics is a sign of unrecognized and unhealed developmental traumas. By using the Two Lists writing exercise, you can begin to identify and clear many of them. It is truly possible over time to clear them from your nervous system, brain and behavioral responses.

We also suggest reading our books, *Breaking Free of the Co-dependency Trap* (2008a) and *The Flight from Intimacy* (2008b). They contain a wealth of information about early childhood trauma during the bonding and separation stages of development. The first part of each book talks about the theory and the problem, and the second part describes how to heal underlying issues.

We also developed the Trauma Elimination Technique (TET) and find it to be a highly effective tool, primarily because it allows you to take charge of your own healing process. We also like it because you do not need to pay a therapist to help you to clear your trauma. This empowering aspect is really important, for most people who have been traumatized also feel disempowered, helpless and powerless.

We developed TET by synthesizing the best of a number of trauma healing modalities: the Tapas Acupressure Technique (TAT), Eye Movement Desensitization and Reprocessing (EMDR), and Thought Field Therapy (TFT). In our extensive use of TET on ourselves and with our clients, we discovered that it not only helps clear trauma from present-life experiences but also from past-life and parallel-life trauma.

The multidimensional potential of TET for clearing trauma from alternate realities is really important. We've discovered that many people are now aware of the karmic nature of their present-life traumas.

If you wish to use TET to clear traumas held in other realities, just set this intention before you begin to use it. If this idea intimidates you, set your intention to clear only present-life trauma. You are always in charge of how you use TET.

TRAUMA ELIMINATION TECHNIQUE

Step 1: Learn the TET holding pose (see photos below).

a) Use one hand to hold three points on your face, as follows. Touch the points lightly.

b) Touch thumb lightly just above and adjacent to the inner corner of one eye.

c) Place the end of your ring (4th) finger just above and adjacent to the inner corner of the other eye.

d) Place the end of your index finger on the indentation in the middle of your forehead, about ½" higher than your eyebrows.

e) Place your other hand palm down at the back of your head, just below the bump at the bottom of your skull (the occipital ridge), center it at the midline.

f) Once you have become comfortable with this pose, go to Step 2.

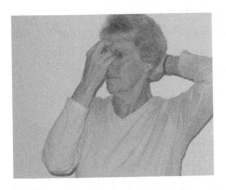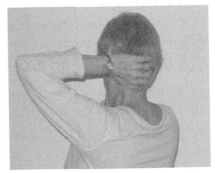

Figure 9.1: The TET Holding Pose

Step 2: If you wish to work on trauma from the past and are not presently in a trauma state, identify a trauma you want to work on. This should be one particular trauma, not one that is long-term or recurring. If you are already in a trauma state, skip to Step 3.

a) Focus your attention on an image related to this trauma.

b) Identify the thoughts that come to you when you view this image.

c) Identify the belief about yourself that goes with this image.

d) Notice what emotion you feel when you see this image, think these thoughts, believe this belief.

Step 3: Simultaneously hold the image, thoughts, belief and feelings related to your traumatic experience while doing the TET holding pose. You do not need to keep dwelling on these aspects; just have the awareness that they are there. Remain in this pose until you feel something happen internally or for one minute, which ever comes first. The internal shift is different for each person, perhaps bringing a subtle shift of energy, a feeling of relaxation, a deep sigh, etc.

Step 4: After this felt sensory shift, scan your body to find where you have been holding tension in your body related to this trauma. Continue to hold the TET pose. Without dwelling on the location of this body tension, hold this pose until you feel another sensory shift, or for one minute.

Step 5: Now return to the image part of your trauma and zoom in close to review it with a magnifying glass, looking for hot spots or things in it that still upset you. This might be someone's facial expression, something in the environment, or anything that still gives you an adrenalin rush.

Step 5: Zero in on this hot spot.

a) Focus on the image, thought, belief, and feeling.

b) Continue the TET holding technique until you feel a shift, or for one minute.

c) Focus on the place in your body where you hold tension related to this memory. Continue the TET holding technique until you experience a felt shift, a body sensation of release or a sigh, or for one minute.

Step 6: Continue returning to the original image and reviewing it until there are no more hot spots.

Step 7: Drink a glass of water immediately after completing a session. Be sure to drink another eight glasses in the next 24 hours to help the toxins released by the TET procedure to leave your body.

Step 8: Sometimes clearing one layer of trauma reveals another layer underneath it. If other layers emerge over the next few days, continue to use the TET protocol.

Once you've cleared one trauma, another may come to the surface that is connected to the first one. For example, if you process a memory that involved your watching your brother get hit with a belt, you might process the part of the trauma that involved your brother yelling as he was hit. Then you might remember the look on his face as he was being struck.

Remembering trauma in layers is pretty common, so don't worry if this happens. If you start having memories that seem overwhelming to process alone, then have someone sit with you while you do the TET, or find a trauma-informed therapist.

CHAPTER TWELVE

HOW TO EXIT THE DRAMA TRIANGLE

"If you actively do something,
it will stop making you feel like a victim
and you'll start feeling like part of the solution,
which is just a huge benefit to your body and your psyche."

—*Ted Danson*

Karpman says that the exit point in the Drama Triangle involves encountering the Persecutors. Once you decide to get off the Triangle, you will be perceived as the Bad Guy. The other game players will feel angry, hurt and rejected because you are leaving them and the pseudo-intimacy you've had together. You must learn how to accept them making you bad. This is critical if you are to break free of the clutches of the Triangle.

ENCOUNTERING THE COKE MACHINE SYNDROME

When you attempt to exit the Drama Triangle, you will likely encounter what we call the Coke Machine Syndrome. This metaphoric game is similar to putting your money in a soda machine and pushing a certain button with the expectation that you'll get the soda of your choice.

If you push the button and nothing happens, however, you might push it again, harder. You might assume the machine is out of your favorite soda and try pushing another button.

If these options don't work, you might try pushing a third or fourth button. And if you are really thirsty, you might push all the buttons. If none of those actions gets you what you want, you might resort to pounding and shaking the machine or cursing at it. Eventually you try pushing the coin return. If that doesn't work, you leave and search for another machine.

Those with whom you play on the Triangle know exactly what your buttons are. As soon as you declare that you are exiting the game, they will begin pushing your buttons, hoping you will re-engage them in their games.

If they don't get the response they want from you, they'll keep pushing different buttons until they realize you will not give them what they want, which is to rejoin the game. Then they will see you as a bad person, declare you a traitor or some other terrible thing, and seek another Coke-Machine person.

Staying off the Drama Triangle requires that you become nonreactive and ungoverned by other people's button-pushing efforts. You must learn how to experience nonreactivity and a less anxious presence, particularly when you are being blamed for something. This is one of the buttons your game-playing friends will surely push.

One way to sidestep the angry and blaming button-pushing messages they direct at you is to make one of the following two comments. You can say to them, *"Thank you, I am aware of that"* or *"Thank you, I wasn't aware of that."* That's all you need to say, and you can repeat it like a broken record if you need to. Take our word for it, this works!

You can also use reflective listening and other communication skills that acknowledge other people's feelings. For example, you could say, *"You seem angry at me because I am not willing to give you money to support your drinking habit."* This helps you sidestep being blamed, feeling guilty, or being manipulated back into the Rescuer role.

HOW TO STOP THE BLAME GAME

An excellent blame-and-drama-stopper statement is, "Is there something that you want from me?" This helps people shift their focus away from blaming and complaining, and toward taking responsibility for their emotions. It requires them to shift from their emotional brain to their thinking brain.

Having to ask directly for what they want is not part of the game and it gives you the opportunity to choose how to respond to their request. If they say, "I don't know," respond with, *"Well think about it and get back to me."*

If they do ask for something, you can say no, giving them your reasons for refusing them. These are straightforward transactions that leave no room for discussion, manipulation, enabling or game playing.

Staying off the Drama Triangle also requires that you learn how to use your own emotions effectively and honestly. You must acknowledge and experience your emotions so others cannot use them to subvert, govern and control your behavior. For example, if you carry around unprocessed anger, it's easy for someone to provoke an angry outburst.

Suppressing emotions is a primary cause of panic attacks, anxieties, compulsions, depression and addictive behaviors. A goal in families is finding a balance point between:

creating a safe space where people can express authentic feelings		not using emotions to manipulate or control others

Most people need help identifying and naming their strong feelings because they are usually associated with unmet needs. Anger, for example, means there's something I want and need that I'm not getting. Sadness means I've lost something important to me and I need comfort. Fear means I don't feel safe and I need protection.

When you are feeling hurt, sad or afraid, it's important to say so. Here's an example of honest communication: "I don't believe you heard me. Would you please listen to what I am saying and repeat it back to me so I know you heard me?" If you do that, people will respond more authentically and honestly.

Once you decide to exit the Drama Triangle and feel strong enough to tolerate being the bad guy, you become a role model for others who also want out of the game. It's important that you not align with those who are leaving the Drama Triangle by making the others still playing on the Traingle bad. That can create a new team of players and start a new Drama Triangle.

BE WILLING TO ASK DIRECTLY FOR WHAT YOU WANT

The primary way to get off the Triangle and stay off is by being willing to ask for what you want from others directly, 100 percent of the time. You must take responsibility for getting your own needs met. You must also make sure that you do not do something for, or give something to, another person unless they have asked you for it or you have asked their permission. This prevents Rescuing and enabling.

If you would like to give something to another person who has not asked for it, you can ask, *"You look like you could use a hug. Would you like a hug?"*

Focus on asking directly for what you want, staying grounded in your own inner experience, and listening to other people's feelings. If you get off-center, take a time-out from the intensity by taking a deep breath and going inside. Remember that what keeps you playing on the Drama Triangle is competition for the Victim role, where you don't ask for what you want.

If you remain committed to asking directly for what you want, 100 percent of the time, you will be able to resist temptations to return to the Drama Triangle.

If you find yourself drawn into a Drama Triangle at work or in your relationships, excuse yourself and take a time-out immediately. Try to identify which role you usually enter the Triangle — Rescuer, Persecutor or Victim — and why. This will help you see where you are vulnerable to Triangle dynamics

.

CHAPTER THIRTEEN

THE FUNCTIONAL FAMILY TRIANGLE

"If you cannot get rid of the family skeleton,
you may as well make it dance."

—*George Bernard Shaw*

There is an alternative to the dysfunctional Drama Triangle: the Functional Family Triangle. When both parents decide to break free of the Drama Triangle by applying the five-step process we share here, it is possible to create a healthy family structure in which everyone communicates directly to get their needs met.

The illustration below shows a Functional Family Triangle. The arrows show that all three sides of the Triangle are in communication with each other. This is what prevents game-playing and drama.

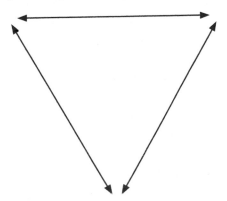

With this kind of healthy social and emotional support, children quickly learn how to get their needs met directly without resorting to manipulation and game-playing. Direct interpersonal communication also helps children heal their natural good/bad splits, and to see themselves and others as *I'm*

okay and you're okay. This is the critical psychological marker that indicates a person has completed their psychological birth and is moving through the individuation process.

Once children are able to operate on internal power, they can use their emotions and inner resources to direct their lives. With the support of a Functional Family Triangle, children can also learn to regulate their emotions and move into the independent stage of development. They have a Self separate from their parents.

FUNCTIONAL FAMILY COMMUNICATIONS SKILLS

Here are some guidelines to help kids and adult children create a Functional Family Triangle. The language we use in these guidelines may initially sound and feel awkward, but it works quite effectively. The process described below usually happens when the child is between 18-24 months old.

1. When an adult caregiver isn't available to meet the child's needs and the child complains or gets upset, do and say the following:

- Support the child's feelings. *"I can see that you are upset because your daddy left."*
- Refuse to participate in the child's judgment about the badness of the unavailable parent, but offer empathy to the child. *"It's hard when you don't see your daddy all day. You'd like him to stay here with you."*
- Reassure the child that his or her needs will be met. *"I'm here to take care of you while your daddy is at work today."*
- Inform the child that the missing caregiver will return. *"Your daddy will be back at four o'clock to pick you up and take you home."*
- Inform the returning caregiver about the child's reaction to the separation. *"Kevin was sad today when you had to leave. He wished that you could be with him all day today."*

2. The returning caregiver should do the following:

- Ask the child if this is true. *"Were you upset that I had to leave? Did you want me to stay with you today?"*
- Support the child's feelings and offer closeness. *"You were sad and mad today because you missed me, right?"*

74

- Express his or her own feelings about separation. *"I miss being with you, too. I feel sad when I have to go to work and leave you. Do you need anything from me right now?"*
- Give the child reasons for the absence. *"Daddy has to go to work to earn money to help pay for the things we need."*

3. When the child has a conflict with one caregiver and brings the conflict to the second caregiver, the second caregiver should do the following:

- Support the child's feelings. *"I can see that you are upset with your mother. You look angry. Are you angry?"*
- Do not agree or disagree with the child's judgment about the first caregiver's badness, but instead offer empathy to the child. *"You are angry because your mother made you clean up your toys. You don't like to pick up your toys."*
- Support the child in dealing directly with the first caregiver to resolve the conflict. *"Are you willing to tell her how you feel?"*
- Help the child talk to first caregiver. *"Do you need any help from me when you go talk to your mother?"*
- Let the child know it's not okay to triangulate and create family secrets. *"If you are not willing to tell her how you feel, I will tell her that you are upset about your conflict with her."*
- Let the child know that you will not resolve his or her conflict with the first caregiver and that you are available to support both the child and the first caregiver when they are ready to resolve it. *"I do not want to get in the middle of this conflict between you and your mother. I will not go to your mother and speak for you. I will only let her know that I am aware you are angry with her. If the two of you want to talk about this, I am available to support both of you."*
- Inform the child that if he or she resolves the conflict without you, you would like to know how it turns out. *"When you and your mother talk about your feelings about having to pick up your toys, please let me know what happens."*

While this kind of communication structure is designed to help young children, it is also highly effective in helping adults whose Inner Child still needs support with separation issues. This kind of clear communication may feel awkward when you first begin using it. Awkwardness is normal when you are in a learning curve. The truth is, we are all in a learning curve about understanding the kind of support young children and adult children need to successfully complete the individuation process.

Very few people have ever experienced this kind of emotional support and clear communication on schedule. When you do use these guidelines, however, you will see how effective they are in helping your children feel accepted and understood.

DYSFUNCTIONAL FAMILY COMMUNICATIONS

Here's a different set of communication guidelines showing what <u>not</u> to do with both young children and adult children.

- Do not contribute to making anyone a bad guy. *"He is never here when you need him."*
- Do not take sides. *"You are right. He doesn't care about you. He doesn't care about anyone."*
- Do not ignore or discount feelings. *"Don't cry. Here, have a cookie."*
- Do not discount the importance of the child's situation. *"I'm busy. Go play."*
- Do not create secrets. *"I won't tell her you are angry at her."*
- Do not rescue. *"I'll talk to your mother and tell her that you shouldn't have to pick up your toys."*
- Do not play the two-against-one Drama Triangle game. *"Let's go talk to your mother. We'll tell her that you shouldn't have to pick up your toys."*

Using both sets of these guidelines will help you and everyone around you create a Functional Family Triangle and break free of Victim Consciousness. If you find yourself saying or doing any of these dysfunctional things, it is never too late to go back and do it differently.

Since most of us still have unresolved issues about becoming emotionally separate, you can use these communication guidelines in your adult relationships where these same two-year-old dynamics are present.

CHAPTER FOURTEEN

HOW TO TAKE CHARGE OF YOUR LIFE

*"When you take charge of your life, there is no longer a need
to ask permission of other people or society at large. When you
ask permission, you give someone veto power over your life."*

—*Geoffrey F. Albert*

Your Shadow, which you may view with fear and disdain, is just your own Divine Inner Child. That awful closet full of monsters or the shame bag you've been dragging all these years. It's just the parts of your inner child that you've split off and hidden.

When you try to protect yourself by hiding these things from others, you also hide them from yourself. When you realize how much you have lost touch with your inner child, you may feel sad and even weep about what you have lost. Once you can mourn the loss of your true self or your inner child, then and only then can you begin the often scary and sometimes painful process of reclaiming those parts of yourself — the parts that you cast aside in order to please others.

Recovering your Divine Inner Child requires facing your weaknesses, insecurities, fears and Shadow parts, and then learning to love each one of those parts as you would love a hurt and rejected child. We often suggest that our clients get a doll, teddy bear or stuffed animal as a symbol of their divine inner child and their split-off parts. Holding this bear, doll or stuffed animal and saying loving things to it can help you love parts of you that people may have told you were unlovable, bad or unacceptable.

TAKE CHARGE OF YOUR LIFE

Most people are walking cases of suppressed happiness trapped in the sticky web of Victim Consciousness. The good news is that you have choices.

Choose to do something about it. Commit to a process of change. Deliberate on how you will make the actual change, set your intention, write your plan and then DO it.

Commit to stop Rescuing others, and listen to your true self. Stop when you find yourself complaining and sounding like a Victim. Refuse to let others Rescue you, and stop listening to their complaints. It's very similar to breaking an addiction — it requires commitment and focus.

Ask directly for what you want from others. When people complain, change the subject and walk away, or ask them, "What do you want from me?" Vow that you won't be dragged into the middle of other people's dramas and mind-games.

You can also look at your current problems with fresh eyes. Make a list of the pros and cons of your life situation. Find a neutral third party to help you review your list — someone who doesn't work where you do, hasn't heard your sad stories before, and isn't related to you. Listen to this person's opinion and don't argue with them if it's not the same as yours.

The goal is to become more objective about your situation and develop a plan to change it. How you change it is up to you. The important things are the plan and proceeding with that plan. The goal is to get moving and to keep taking small daily steps that move you in the direction of self-responsibility.

If you find yourself in relationships involving three or more people, like a family, use healthy communication interactions based on the Functional Family Triangle. Healthy relationships require that all the people involved interact with each other. This prevents secrets, gossiping, power plays and two-against-one games, while also building safety, trust and intimacy.

The bad news is that it is very difficult to break free of Victim Consciousness and the Drama Triangle without alienating some who are close to you. When you decide to stop being a Victim and begin asking directly for what you want, you will be exiting from dysfunctional, often unconscious, relationship agreements that may go back generations.

Be aware that others close to you may interpret your departure from the Triangle as a personal rejection. They may feel hurt and even be depressed when you refuse to participate in this crippled form of intimacy. Others may become angry and attack you. They may even try to turn those you care about against you by spreading rumors or telling lies about you. While this won't get them what they want — being close to you — it will attract other people to replace you on the Triangle. It may also get them some Victim payoffs via the Coke Machine Syndrome.

Prepare for these challenges when you decide to stop giving the pay-off that people typically get from you via the Drama Triangle. They will push your customary buttons harder. If that doesn't work, eventually they will look for other buttons to push.

They may yell at you, try to shame you or try to make you feel guilty. If this doesn't get them what they want, they may tell others what a bad person you are. Ultimately, if you don't play on the Triangle with them, they will go away in search of others who will.

Getting off the Triangle takes courage and strength. It isn't easy enduring the barbs thrown at you by others who say you are rejecting or abandoning them.

Remember that one key to breaking free of the Drama Triangle and Victim Consciousness is reflecting back people's feelings when they complain or accuse you. This tells them that you care about them. Asking them what they want from you is also an effective drama-stopper. They have to stop whining and complaining, and think about what they want from you. Usually they don't even know.

If they don't know what they want from you, ask them to think about it and tell you when they do know. If they do know what they want or need, they will have to ask directly for it. This actually brings the Drama Triangle to a screeching halt.

Sometimes you don't get opportunities to connect in a compassionate way. In these cases, we suggest viewing those who seek to pull you back onto the Triangle as wounded in some way. Hold them in your heart while they struggle with Victim Consciousness. Believe that they can break free, and hold this vision for them. This kind of support can be a really powerful force in helping them without your having to play on the Drama Triangle.

We send you our support and caring on your journey. Please let us know about your progress and your success stories via the contact form that appears on our website, www.weinholds.org.

Made in the USA
Middletown, DE
13 February 2022